Medjugorje

My Lifelong Journey with
Our Lady, Queen of Peace

Penny Abbruzzese

En Route Books and Media, LLC
St. Louis, MO

ENROUTE
Make the time

En Route Books and Media, LLC
5705 Rhodes Avenue
St. Louis, MO 63109

Contact us at contactus@enroutebooksandmedia.com

Cover credit: Penny Abbruzzese with the assistance of Rosemarie
Ruiz and Diana Barone

ISBN-13: 978-1-956715-03-3 (paperback)
ISBN-13: 978-1-956715-14-9 (hardback)

Library of Congress Control Number: 2021949247

This book is dedicated to

Our Lady…

Our Life, Our Sweetness, and Our Hope

Contents

Acknowledgments

I met Father Svetozar Kraljevic, OFM, on my first pilgrimage to Medjugorje in March, 1984. I wrote my conversion story under his direction in 1987. Father Svet was my sole contact with the ongoing events. Although I struggled to write, I did as Father suggested and through the grace of God, I finished my fourteenth chapter in seven months. I titled that book *About a Mother, by a Mother... Thank You Mary, Queen of Peace*. My book included a foreword by Dr. Fr. Tomislav Pervan, OFM, pastor of the Church of St. James in Medjugorje from 1982-1988.

I sent my manuscript to several Catholic publishers and then I waited. Polite letters of rejection began to arrive—all stating that the market was flooded with books on Medjugorje. I was very much at peace with these circumstances; however, I would leave my transformation story, from darkness into light through Our Lady's intercession, for my children and grandchildren to read one day.

It was surely God's timing that my book was not published so many years ago. I clearly see that those years were meant to focus on my husband and family. God calls us to serve while serving our primary vocations, and mine was wife and mother.

The fruits of my story are only possible because of the wonderful people with whom God has blessed me. I will let God, through Our Lady, bestow His graces on so many unnamed friends and family for their help and continuous support. I wish to thank some, however, who contributed to making this work a reality—starting with my mom and dad and my four precious siblings.

I thank God for my wonderful husband, Mike; our three beautiful children, Lori, Michael, and Donna; their spouses, Gregory, Jeanine, and Stephen; and my priceless grandchildren: Sofia, Trey, Tristen, Sienna, James, and Antonio.

Mike and I celebrated our 50th Wedding Anniversary in October, 2020. Of the many guests I planned to invite, most are like family since we have traveled together on countless pilgrimages. I have been blessed to make these through the hard work and generosity of my most cherished friend, Milanka Lachman. Milanka is the founder and President of 206 Tours. She and her amazing staff have organized each and every one of the hundred plus pilgrimages that I have undertaken since 1987.

In March, 2019, Mike and I were invited to Milanka's house for a small dinner party. I was shocked when Milanka and her husband Charlie opened the doors to their living room and there stood over eighty guests, including all of our grandchildren, who yelled "SURPRISE!" for my 70th birthday! That evening will always be one of my most beloved memories. I felt embraced by God's divine love. It was like crossing over from this life into Heaven!

Thanks also to my dear friend, Cathy Hammill. Cathy accompanied me on my third pilgrimage to Medjugorje in December, 1985. Since then, Cathy has been my right arm in most of my endeavors: starting prayer groups for priests and for families, encouraging our newsletter, and helping to finance our documentary. The list goes on even today.

Always with Cathy was her supportive husband, Greg, and their six daughters, one of whom is Christine Hammill-Cregan. Christine lovingly took each chapter and very gently corrected my inverted thoughts and run-on sentences without missing one heartbeat of my story. Christine, her husband Anthony, and her sisters have always been there for me; each one with an immense devotion to Our Lady.

My deepest thanks also to Gigi Hayes for editing my book with leniency and sensitivity. Gigi and her husband Rich are active members of the Parish of St. Agnes Cathedral. Gigi is a member of a prayer group who call themselves the Disciples of Divine Mercy, also known as the DDM's. Gigi was my discussion group leader years ago when the DDM's introduced to our Cathedral Parish a program based on the book *33 Days to Morning* Glory by Father Michael E. Gaitley, MIC. The DDM's brought nearly 260 parishioners closer to Jesus through Mary, as part of the Hearts of Fire Series. For six weeks, Gigi, Mary Tierney, and the rest of the team of DDM's prepared us to consecrate ourselves to Our Lady. The members of the DDM's are among my closest friends and without their prayer support, love, and friendship, I would be a fish out of water.

To those of you mentioned in my story, I express my gratitude for your invaluable friendship. I hope I have reported our time together with sincerity and love.

I am eternally grateful to the Holy Priesthood. I am blessed to take the names of over 500 priests to Adoration daily. Without them, we would not have Jesus in the Eucharist, which is my lifeline and daily sustenance.

My heartfelt gratitude is to Our Lord and Our Lady for being so patient with me. They pick me up with love every time I fall. They brush me off and put me back on the right track with weekly confession. They give me a spiritual hug, as I press the reset button and begin again. I thank them for allowing me to take you, dear reader, on this spiritual journey.

I take full responsibility for the way I express myself, and the accuracy of the content rests entirely with me.

Update on the Status of Medjugorje by Pope Francis

Cited by Catholic News Agency, May 12, 2019

"Pope Francis has given the green light for Catholics to organize pilgrimages to Medjugorje, a site of alleged Marian apparitions, though the Church has not yet given a verdict on the apparitions' authenticity."

The pope's authorization of pilgrimages to the site is not to be understood as an "authentication" of the alleged apparitions, "which still require an examination by the Church," papal spokesman Alessandro Gisotti said in a statement May 12th.

He added that anyone leading pilgrimages to the site should avoid creating "confusion or ambiguity under the doctrinal aspect" including priests who intend to celebrate Mass there.

The provision was made as an acknowledgement of the "abundant fruits of grace" that have come from Medjugorje and to promote those "good fruits." It is also part of the "particular pastoral attention" of Pope Francis to the place, Gisotti said.

The announcement of the papal authorization was made May 12th by the Vatican's apostolic visitor to the site, apostolic nuncio to Bosnia and Herzegovina, Archbishop Henryk Hoser, and Archbishop Luigi Pezzuto.

Archbishop Hoser, retired archbishop of Warsaw-Prague, was appointed apostolic visitor to Medjugorje by Pope Francis in May 2018. His directive, which was of an undetermined length, was to oversee the pastoral needs at the site of the alleged Marian apparitions. Archbishop Hoser's appointment as apostolic visitor followed his service as papal envoy to the site in 2017. He passed to Eternal life on August 13, 2021.

***In conformity to Pope Urban VIII's Decree and the directives of the Council Vatican II, the author declares not to have the intention to precede the judgement of the Church, to whom she submits herself fully. Words like "apparitions," "messages," and others of a similar meaning, have here the value of human witness. ***

In the wake of my plan to finish my writing in 2019, which I began in 1987, I felt in my heart that God has something else for me to add. The coronavirus epidemic was unexpected, and although I could write an entire chapter on three months of quarantine in 2020, with its trials and graces, I will not. The sad report is that on April 10, 2020, 799 people in New York died from coronavirus in a single 24-hour period captures the magnitude of the experience. Our Lady's latest message from Medjugorje, June 25, 2020, which I found most profound and urgent, reflects our current times.

"Dear children! I am listening to your cries and prayers, and am interceding for you before my Son Jesus, who is the Way, the Truth and the Life. Return, little children to prayer and open your hearts in this time of grace and set out on the way of conversion. Your life is passing and,

without God, does not have meaning. This is why I am with you to lead you towards holiness of life, so that each of you may discover the joy of living. I love you all, little children, and am blessing you with my motherly blessing. Thank you for having responded to my call."

FOREWORD

by Dr. Fr. Tomislav Pervan, O.F.M., Pastor of St. James in Medjugorje since August, 1982 until October, 1988

The work we have before us is the fruit of a long spiritual journey. It is a search for the path of life and a way out of the tunnel of fears, doubts, and enslavement into freedom, grace, new birth, and new life, like the fruit of a long-lasting search. This book is written through the eyes of a mother who carefully observes Mary, the Mother; through the eyes of a wife who keeps ever before her the humble Handmaiden of Her husband and God's Son.

This book embodies in itself an everyday life which is a portrayal of countless contemporary lives. That life is literally a picture, a symbol. Everyone's life in modern times is a life full of fears and dependencies – a life in which people pay homage to the idols of today which, even though they do not wish it, enslave and dominate them.

This book is a book of honest search, of tireless pilgrimage not only of the body, but of the spirit and heart, too. Everyone must travel that interior path and road of purification in order to depart from the world of fear, slavery, and dependency and enter the world of the freedom of God's children. Mary walked that way and Mary stands before us as a model.

The same way is made clearly visible from the vivid experiences of a simple mother who straight-forwardly describes the events of her life. We see arising before us a contemporary witness of the message of Jesus Christ for today's world. Before us is being opened the way out of that foreign land into the homeland, a way full of internal and external dangers, even despair, bitterness, discouragement, sacrifice, and renunciation. Nothing advances in a straight line. Nothing can be foreseen ahead of time. One must surrender to Divine Providence and cooperate with it. It is learning from Mary how God confidently and safely leads us. It is learning that it is not we who are fashioning life and history, but rather to live in God and out of God. And no matter what may have happened to us on this path of life, one thing is clear – God is on our side! He is "Emmanuel," "God with us." Even in our interior and exterior anxieties, difficulties, and troubles. Out of all this it becomes very clear that the greatest grace and happiness is to be human and to grow into a human being having God "at his right hand" as an ever-present help and protection and having Mary as a model and safe guide. For, if God exists, if God is among us in Jesus Christ, then it makes no sense whatsoever to live in fear, to be people of fear, or to be enslaved by others out of fear. If God is with us, then already here on earth is the beginning of Heaven, even if only in the form of an embryo, a seed, a nucleus.

Our author has experienced this in coming to Medjugorje and in "living Medjugorje" in her home, in the circle of her friends, carrying forth the messages of Medjugorje into a concrete life situation. For Mary is here in the name of entire humanity which needs help, which needs redemption and a Redeemer. She is here in Medjugorje as a living and present symbol of all that is in us which longs for freedom, humanity, salvation, and redemption. She is the advocate of a fallen mankind which daily relives "the fall," the original sin of our first parents, continuously indulging "carnal allurements, enticements for eye, the life of empty show." (1 Jn 2:16) Before Her and Her Son, Jesus Christ, it becomes very clear to us what we should like to be and what we should actualize in our lives: to be free of those "original sins" of mankind, to live like human beings, to believe and surrender ourselves, to be born as human beings, and to be reborn in the Holy Spirit. "God's planting, God's offspring, the work of God's hands, that He be glorified in us." (Is 60:21) Each one of us carries within that call which the Lord has planted in us when, creating us, He sent us into this world. The image of the Mother with the child Jesus is a universal permission to decide ultimately and to begin to be that which we are: children who yearn for the Kingdom of God. Jesus was not able to offer us a more perfect and simple image by which to grasp His Kingdom, His Lordship, than that of mere children, of little ones.

Something of that littleness is reflected in this effort, an effort to walk daily after the Lord, to imitate Jesus guided by the sure hand of the Mother who has only one goal: to lead everyone to Her Son, to direct us on the only safe way promising the future. And that way is the Gospel, the Good News to the entire universe that God exists, that God rejoices over mankind and because of mankind, that God is happy over our happiness and unhappy over our unhappiness and our rushing headlong into self-willed catastrophe. But the Mother is here to turn back the Evil One from Her children. May God grant us the grace to hear this message in the following pages.

Chapter One

My Own Little World

In hoping to achieve the nearly ineffable task of sharing how the supernatural presence of the Blessed Mother here on Earth has brought me to rediscover my faith, I take you first to a tree-lined street in Brooklyn where memories are rooted and a sibling love bloomed.

It was like yesterday, that Saturday morning. I was five years old and excited about moving into our new house, but only for the first two days. Then Monday came along. My dad was back to work, my older brother and sister went off to their new school, and mom was buried in mounds of boxes. That's when I discovered my new playmate and soon-to-be best friend, my brother Chucky. We explored this new neighborhood together, the two of us, Chucky in his white police car, and I on foot. Chucky was three years old, and he was told to stay close to me. That bond knitted us as a team. When it finally was my turn to go to school, leaving Chucky behind was what I found the most difficult. I could not wait to get home in the afternoon to catch up on what we had missed together.

Without planning it, we reserved every Saturday to be with one another, from early morning cartoons until dusk. Time went on and we became good friends with other children on the block, but the knitted bond between Chucky and me stitched tighter and tighter even as we enjoyed the same circle of friends. Mom's words to us when we were five and three, "Stay close together," seemed to be our unconscious guideline.

Chucky and I fought like cats and dogs when we were twelve and ten, and the only solution that saved us from killing each other was not to talk to each other for a whole year. I would not recommend this to every brother and sister who are at each other's throats, but for Chucky and me, it became the only way to give our parents a break from our constant bickering. Once during the year, I suggested a pact that allowed us to talk on holidays. Mom and Dad weren't thrilled with what was going on, but it worked. When the year ended, it was as if our arguments had never existed. I never fought with Chucky again.

My two sisters, Judi and Susan, and my brother, Bobby, were very dear to me. For some reason, though, it was always Chucky and I who paired off together. When I was sixteen and working as a cashier in a supermarket, I received my first paycheck. I had no intention of spending my little fortune in any particular way, but on the way home, I found myself stopping in a jewelry store to buy a Head of Christ medal for Chucky. It left me with only a few dollars, but with such a proud feeling. The medal wasn't indicative of my religious convictions. Rather, it was simply a symbol of love for my best friend who used to ride alongside me in his white police car.

We double-dated throughout the years, and we stayed close after marriage. We shared a love for each other's spouses. When Chucky was at work, it was my own husband, Mike who rushed Chucky's wife to the hospital to deliver her second born. Our families were an extension of our bond of friendship. I rejoiced in this beautiful part of my own little world.

No one's journey of faith is without crosses to carry. My journey is no different, and I was soon to carry my own heavy cross. I said good night to Chucky on Thanksgiving evening, 1982. I wonder to this day if he knew in his heart that it would be our last time together. I thought I knew my brother inside and out. The real truth is that I did not. That Chucky should even think of taking his own life three days later was, and still is, inconceivable. Yet, he did.

November 28, 1982, is the day that my own little world collapsed and a part of me died. I had just returned from 4:30 p.m. Mass with my three young children, Lori, Michael, and Donna. My husband, Mike, a police officer, was working the four to midnight shift. The phone rang. I knew something was wrong as soon as I heard an obvious quiver in my mother's voice. After a brief pause, she said, "Chucky's car was found on the Bayonne Bridge early this morning." The

Bayonne Bridge connects Staten Island, a borough of New York City, with New Jersey. Chucky's car had been left in the middle of the bridge with its motor running and the keys in the ignition.

Chucky was supposed to be at his job for the Transit Authority in the borough of Brooklyn that morning, not in New Jersey. There was no note and no sign of him anywhere. I naively questioned, "What was he doing on the bridge? Where is he now?" I wanted to think that his car broke down, and he went for help. When my mother said that the police seemed to think he jumped, I couldn't help but cry, "Why? Why would he do that?" I didn't have to call the children together; they were at my side. They knew something was very, very wrong. My thought was to call Mike. He'd find Chucky, and this nightmare would be over. It didn't work out that way.

Immediately, we all felt the need to search for Chucky. My brother, Bobby, and Mike tried to put their pain aside amidst all the confusion and investigate. This was their job. This was what they both did as detectives in the New York City Police Department. I can never describe what it must have been like for Bobby and Mike to do the best job possible. They had to put their emotions on hold. Bobby and Mike showed Chucky's picture to local motel clerks. We all looked up and down streets and in every nook and cranny in Bayonne, New Jersey. We left his picture with the Bayonne Police. We hoped someone might see him. It got dark. Bobby had to drive Chucky's car home from the bridge. The memory of following Bobby driving Chucky's car summons a pain I wish I could forget. As I drove, I fixed my eyes on a capless driver. Chucky always wore a cap.

There were many times in my dad's life in which he felt that God forewarned him of imminent danger with life-like dreams. One early morning at 4 a.m. dad awakened with a dream of a fire at my sister Judi's house. It was the exact time Judi's son, Tommy, was shaken out of bed. Tommy's bedspread rested on the bulb of a lamp that had been left on, and his bedspread began to flame.

With Chucky's disappearance, my sister Judi and my dad were visibly dying inside. They both tried to be strong for one another. Though Dad knew it was hopeless to look for his son, he kept that feeling to himself. The night before, he had seen Chucky in a dream. Dad could see Chucky in the distance ascending towards the clouds. Dad's belief that these dreams were from God was unwavering. He knew his son was not coming back.

My dad and Judi went into the Bridge Authority headquarters with Bobby and Mike. My mother and I waited in the car. We were both very still until the others disappeared from sight. Then I just folded into my mother's arms like a small child. Amid the tears, there were no words, but the silent breaking of our hearts was deafening.

During the month of December, I vacillated between clinging to rays of hope and wandering through tunnels of darkness. Several family members went to a medium who said that Chucky was alive, but scared. It appeared that Chucky's credit card had been used to buy new jeans, but we found out days later that the store was only late in sending the bill. Friends from work confirmed what Chucky told us on Thanksgiving; that a colleague's brother held a grudge against him. As a result of this grudge, we knew Chucky's life had been threatened. Could my brother have been killed or kidnapped?

I went to church, though I found it almost impossible to pray. I asked our Pastor to list Chucky's name with the sick, announcing this at Sunday Mass each week. I had accepted the reality that my brother was mentally sick.

The holidays drew near, and we all anxiously awaited our Christmas Eve gathering at our parents' house in Brooklyn. If Chucky was out there somewhere, tonight would be the night he'd come home. Every time the doorbell rang, our hearts took a spin, but just for a moment. Trying to behave normally, as though nothing was different, my eyes stayed glued to the living room door waiting for my brother to walk through.

The night was still young, and we tried to hold back the hands of time as long as we could. The doorbell rang. Instead of Chucky, it was my brother's friend, Dennis, with whom he had grown up. Dennis brought gifts for Helen, Chucky's wife, and for his young sons, Brian and Stephen. Again, the bell rang. This time it was one of my oldest friends. A neighbor was outside more than in, waiting for Chucky's car to pull up on the block. How ironic it was that friends came to celebrate Christmas with our family, but Chucky wasn't there.

Our hearts were heavy with unspoken grief. It was getting late. The hardest part of all was to leave each other that Christmas Eve night with spirits that were lifeless instead of joyous. Chucky was not coming home for Christmas. He was not coming home at all.

After six weeks of feeling numb, in the beginning of January, 1983, I finally broke down and asked a woman named Helen, with whom I worked, to pray for my brother. Helen always had a special peace about her that radiated as she shared with us an awakening she experienced through her prayer group when she realized God's love for her. I didn't know what a prayer group was. Suddenly, it was important for me to ask Helen if her prayer group would pray for Chucky. Helen said that they had been praying for him from the very beginning. I was so moved by that. I felt a great sense of relief in asking her for their continued prayers. I was angry at God for His silence and couldn't pray, yet I realized it was important that I ask for the prayers of others.

I'll never forget the day of January 10. That afternoon a storm arose, and it continued into the evening. I was at a wake that night with my friends, and we stopped at a diner for a cup of coffee. I felt the need to call my sister Judi. We were all so drained by events of the past six weeks. The calls that we shared almost every evening created a closeness that we had not felt in years. For some reason, Judi's telephone line was busy. I must have tried a dozen times.

I arrived home around eleven. Lori, my oldest, was still awake. She said she couldn't sleep. Donna and Michael were sleeping. Mike was working from four to midnight. He was supposed to sleep over at the precinct that night because his tour the next day started at eight a.m. Suddenly, the phone rang. It was Judi. "Is Mike home yet?" she said. I said he wasn't expected home that night, yet two minutes later she asked the same question. I wondered why. Why did she persist in asking if Mike was home? I pleaded with her to tell me. Finally, she said, "They found Chucky's body this afternoon. It washed up during the storm. Two young boys playing along the shore discovered it."

The last thread was cut. The hope that I held onto with everything I had was gone. I could search the whole world over and never find the words to describe the unbelievable pain of facing the truth. Chucky took his own life, and I would never see him again. I collapsed on the couch in Lori's arms, totally broken.

Mike had received a call from Judi earlier in the evening to tell him that they had found Chucky's body. He was rushing home in that brutal storm to tell me the news himself when his car broke down on the parkway. It was late, and he was completely drenched. I think of how hard it must have been for Mike. Not only having to wait for help with his car, but also the reality that Chucky, who was like a brother to him, was dead.

It was the beginning of my asking, "Why did he do it? Didn't he know what this would do to us? How could he have been so selfish? Why was he planning a winter fishing trip with his boss, and then take his own life that very day? Why didn't he say goodbye?" In his arms that night, I listened as Mike tried to help me understand the agony Chucky must have been in to take his own life. I still asked, "Why?"

Our daughter Donna had slept through all of this and had no idea what was happening. She had a special love for her Uncle Chucky. She and Chucky's son, Brian, are just six weeks apart in age. They already had planned to be law partners together when they grew up. Donna came into our room around two in the morning. Very peacefully, she said, "Uncle Chucky just came though my window with two angels. He said, 'Donna, don't worry, I'm all right.'" I was awestruck by what she was telling me, yet comforted by it.

There is so much more that I wish I could share with you, but to make you understand the pain that my parents and sisters and I went through would be impossible. Yet, there is my brother Bobby's experience that I feel is to be shared.

My brother Bobby was also working the four to midnight shift on the night of January 10. Detectives from Bayonne called Bobby at work and asked him to come over. They told him of a body that had been found that afternoon under the bridge and asked if he would come to identify it. His partners wanted to go with him to the morgue, but Bobby refused. He wanted to go alone. Oh, God, will he ever forget when they uncovered Chucky, and he had no face, just a few stubbles of his beard? His face. His face that I'd begged to see just one more time eroded in the ocean water. The wallet in his new jeans was the only means of identifying him. I pray that someday Bobby will be able to share with me some of his pain in uncovering our brother's body.

The following morning, I took our children to school at St. Raymond's Catholic Elementary and prayed that I would see our pastor. Father Singleton usually stood outside of the school to greet the children before they start their day. "Father," I said, "they found my brother Chucky. He did commit suicide. Can he still go to heaven?" His answer was, "There is no eleventh commandment saying that if you take your own life, you cannot reach heaven."

Thank you, God, for the gift of Father Singleton being right there. For, if his answer to me was without comfort, I do not know if I would have held on to the hope that Chuck wasn't condemned for eternity. In retrospect, I thank you, Lord, for the storm you sent and for answering all of the prayers which were entrusted to you. It is possible that we might never have found my brother's body. Oh, Mary, your Son did give us a gift on January 10. To us, it was death. But for Chucky, as he leapt into God's arms, it was new life!

Chapter Two

A Rude Awakening

A few weeks after Chucky was buried, I read the book *Why Bad Things Happen to Good People* by Rabbi Harold S. Kushner. Rabbi Kushner's view of life's coincidences, or God's providence, prodded my conscience. Did I believe, as he wrote, that every fraction of a second of our day contained a fragment of God's hidden life and secret activity? Like millions of Catholics, I was taught from the Baltimore Catechism that God was everywhere and always with us. But, at this point in time, what I knew in my head and what I felt in my heart seemed to be opposed to one another.

As a product of Catholic upbringing and Catholic school teaching for eight years, I believed in Heaven, Hell, and Purgatory. Aside from my grandmother's dying when I was ten, I had been shielded from any pain of separation. I rarely thought about life after death. Until now. Suddenly, it was imperative for me to know where Chucky was. Was he with God? Prior to his death, Chucky had stopped attending Mass on Sundays. I, too, had become lax in Mass attendance. But I would not be at peace until I felt that Chucky was in Heaven with God.

I knew that I needed to pray more now than I did at any other time in my life. I felt that I needed to do so in case Chucky wasn't in Heaven. I had learned in grammar school that Purgatory was a place where souls suffer for a time after death for sins unatoned for while they were alive. Other than Our Lord and Our Lady, I didn't believe that anyone was without sin. Our Christian doctrine teaches us that we are in communion with the souls in Purgatory and can help them with our prayers and good works. If Chucky needed to depend on my prayers, it worried me because they were just about nonexistent. My prayers were but a passing thought, and I felt he needed more than I was giving.

Mike's sister Karen and I were extremely close because of her first-born child, a beautiful baby boy named David. Karen and her husband, John, hadn't expected David until September of 1982, but a slight car accident brought on delivery in her seventh month of pregnancy.

When Mike's father called to tell us about Karen's delivery, the concern in his voice was alarming. "Karen is fine," he said, "but the baby is not expected to live more than twenty-four hours." David was born with a disease called toxoplasmosis. In its congenital form, it damages the central nervous system, the eyes, and the internal organs of the body, especially the heart, lungs, liver, kidneys, and intestines. David was also diagnosed as having hydrocephalus, or water on the brain. Karen and John were told that if David were to survive, he would be hopelessly handicapped.

We were all stunned. I personally assumed that the baby was going to die. I went shopping to bring something special to the hospital for Karen. I brought several personal gifts, thinking that would make her feel better. I couldn't, or perhaps I selfishly didn't want to, place myself in her position and feel what she was going through. It was too difficult and much too painful. My husband, Mike, found it all overwhelming, and I accepted his denial of David's problems. David was not perfect. Though our hearts ached for Karen and John, we cut ourselves off emotionally from this child. If he were to live, we imagined David would be one heartache after another. I wondered why a child like this would be brought into this world.

David did survive his first twenty-four hours. The doctors told Karen and John that, in time, they would have to operate on David, implanting a shunt in his head to relieve the water pressure that made his head so large. It would need to be redone periodically, depending on how rapidly fluid built up. A month after David was born, Karen and John went to a healing mass in Boston. David immediately began to experience a miraculous healing. His head went down in size and there was no longer the probability that fluid would accumulate again. Without the shunt, this could only have happened through Our Divine Healer. The thought of God's being in control quietly entered my heart.

After ten weeks in the hospital, Karen and John were anxious to bring him home. By this time, my feelings had begun to change. Loving David *just as he was* took hold of my heart. The birth announcement read, "We celebrate the gift of our son, David, who has come to us wrapped in love and clothed in struggle. We ask that you join with us in faith and the joyful realization of God's continued healing presence in our lives. Our prayer is that David be given the strength to sustain and nurture the Great Life that fills him." I began to pray for my new nephew.

When I visited their apartment, I was amazed at how much care this little guy needed, yet it seemed like second nature to Karen and John. It took almost an hour to feed David through a tube, but the love that radiated from them is impossible to describe. And this was repeated numerous times throughout the day. Patience was not one of my virtues. I wondered if I would be able to give that much of myself to someone else, no matter how much I loved them. What a special calling Karen and John had, and what a heavy cross they had been asked to carry.

Shortly after Chucky's death, Karen and I were driving in the car when the conversation led to what each of us was going through. Karen touched on a few of my uncommunicated feelings. She understood my family's pain. It was difficult for me to let down my protective shield. As a family and individually, we were in unbelievable pain. We were overwhelmed with feelings of guilt and asked one another why we couldn't have helped him.

Two blocks before we reached my house, I finally shared with Karen how angry I was with God. Yet, I felt the need to pray for Chucky. I will never forget saying, "I want to pray, Karen. I just don't know the words to say."

My knowledge of God consisted of nightly prayers that lasted thirty seconds at most. Ever since I could remember, each night I would thank God for all that He had done for me. I would say that I was sorry for all the wrong that I had done. I would ask God to bless my family, friends, and relatives. Then, discreetly, so no one would see and know I was praying, I would blow a quick kiss up to Heaven. That was it! Even after Chucky died, I continued my nightly thirty seconds of prayer, though I knew that my feelings were barren and that I felt so insincere.

Karen asked if I had a rosary. I was embarrassed to admit that I hadn't had one since I was in grammar school. I never really prayed to the Blessed Mother except during Mass on Sundays. I recalled saying the Mass in Latin, and if we looked distracted the sisters would come up to us and say, "Pray another rosary." That was the extent of the rosary and Our Lady in my life. Karen gave me her rosary and asked that I say just one decade each day. I made that promise and began that night. Every night following, I would say one decade. One Our Father and ten Hail Marys. From thirty seconds of prayer, I progressed to three minutes each day. That, I could handle.

No sooner did I begin praying when we were faced with another life or death situation. Chucky's five-year-old son, Stephen, began having convulsions and running very high fevers. This had never happened before, and we wondered if it could be from the trauma of losing his dad. My sister-in-law, Helen, had found Stephen on the floor of his room - colorless and shaking out of control. Helen rushed him to the hospital. There he began to vomit. Some vomit went down his throat and began to fill his lungs. He was rushed into Pediatric Intensive Care, and the code was STAT! Helen heard the doctors say, "We're losing him!"

I avoided facing my true feelings and the truth of what was happening around me. In what was probably a sub-conscious attempt to deny the seriousness of what was happening to Stephen, I went to an exercise class before going to the hospital. I could have gone to church and prayed for Stephen, but exercise class, my four-day-a-week ritual, took priority. At this point in time, when I had just allowed God into my life ever so slightly, I was about to close the door once more.

In the hospital room that night, our hearts broke all over again. Stephen was the spitting image of his father. His whole body was wrapped in white sheets ever so tightly to try to control his trembling. All you could see was this precious little face exposed above the sheet. He was quivering. His lips were so chapped and purple that he couldn't talk. And he was terrified.

The next forty-eight hours were critical. Doctors told us that permanent changes might occur in Stephen's nervous system like those of shaking palsy, and he might suffer deterioration in intelligence. I asked God to please help us take one day at a time.

Stephen was diagnosed as having Viral Encephalitis. Encephalitis literally means inflammation of the brain. This virus left him hospitalized for nearly three weeks. Towards the end of his illness, I stayed overnight in the hospital so Helen could get some rest. I felt so blessed to have special time alone with Stephen. There were times while Stephen was sick that I thought God was punishing us by sending us one tragedy after another. But when he fell asleep, I realized that after almost losing Stephen, we should be giving thanks to God for renewing his life. A tremendous sense of God's love uprooted my anxieties and filled me with a newly discovered conviction of His Fatherhood for every single one of us.

It took a year for Stephen's trembling to subside. He was fragile for the longest time. A month after he was home from the hospital, he visited with us overnight. Without warning, he suddenly ran a high fever and soon afterwards began having seizures. Within minutes, I was following the emergency squad to the hospital, but this time I was praying. Stephen was treated and released the following day.

As a result of Stephen's recovery, my three minutes of prayer each day suddenly began to take on new meaning.

The Our Father and the Hail Marys were no longer just words to me. Asking God to "forgive us our trespasses," prompted me to plead for forgiveness for all the times I had turned my back on Him when His arms were outstretched and He wanted so much to show me His love. As I asked Mary to "pray for us sinners," my heart sank because I found myself praying as in a conversation with Our Lady, saying, "Oh Mary, how much longer can I deny God? I know I am a sinner, and I need you to pray for me." I prayed on my knees to Our Lady, pouring out my heart and soul. In emptying myself to Mary, I discovered the comfort of a mother's love. All my life I only knew Mary as the Mother of God. Through my brokenness, Mary was now becoming my Spiritual Mother.

Soon, I couldn't wait for that special time of day when the house was quiet, usually in the afternoon. I would start praying, always imploring Mary to please tell Jesus how sorry I was for not trusting Him and loving Him more. I unintentionally cried, realizing that I had taken God for granted all my life. Mike and I have three beautiful children, and I could not recall even one time of my praying to God that they would be healthy. I simply took those things for granted.

Trying to recite one decade of the rosary seemed almost impossible now. I could not get past the first Hail Mary when my prayers would flow into tears. I did not know what was happening. I never even considered that those tears were a cleansing of my soul. I simply could not hold them back, and to be honest, I didn't want to. More often than not, those three minutes of prayer now took me an hour. I felt so drained after praying, but also felt really good inside.

As I prayed, I worried about whether Chucky was in Heaven. I cried out loud to Our Lady telling her that my heart was breaking. I felt Our Lady share my pain. Mary was listening to my prayers. I persistently prayed, "What can I do to help him?" The following month, in May of 1983, Our Lady answered my prayer. It was a Wednesday afternoon. I had brought my daughter to her track team practice. My best friend, Janet, was on one side of the fence, and I was on the other. Janet told me that the guest speaker at her parish prayer meeting the night before was the District Attorney of Nassau County, Denis Dillon. That drew my attention at once. His talk had been about Our Blessed Mother who was currently appearing every night to six young children in a small village named Medjugorje in Yugoslavia. These nightly appearances, according to the children, had been occurring for almost two years.

Denis told the group that the Blessed Mother was pleading with us to turn from our sins, to reconcile ourselves with God and man, and to strive for peace. Inner peace brought about by personal conversion would then lead to peace in the world. In addition, the Blessed Mother had promised to give a total of ten secrets to the children. A number of these secrets will concern the fate of the world. Our Lady has told the visionaries that the world is on the brink of a major catastrophe caused by the sin within it. This catastrophe cannot be avoided but can be diminished. For this reason, the Blessed Mother urges increased faith, daily prayers, in particular the rosary, monthly confession, sacrifice, and fasting. The Blessed Mother was telling us through these six children that we were to fast on bread and water on Fridays and to offer up all of our sacrifices to God, no matter how small.

As Janet spoke about Our Lady's reported appearances, I felt that her words were meant for me to hear. I didn't have to be convinced that it was real; I believed right away. This was Our Lady's answer to my prayer: to fast on Fridays and turn back to God. Without thinking twice, I decided I was going to do this for my brother.

Two days later was Friday, and I was all set to start. I told Mike about Our Lady and what fasting meant to me and that I would like to try to fast. He had no qualms about my not eating on Fridays, and I thanked God for that. Our children had no doubt that this is what I wanted to do and never questioned my reasoning. I went to work on Friday with my supply for fasting - packs of sugarless gum and sugarless mints. I felt that the only way I could do this was to keep my mouth in motion with something other than real food.

This was all brand new to me, so I did not think to ask for the grace to fast. I had forgotten that grace was something more than just a prayer before meals. We had learned growing up as Catholics that grace was a supernatural gift of

God, freely bestowed upon us for our sanctification and salvation. We were also taught that we obtain God's grace chiefly through prayer and the Holy Sacraments. Thirty years was a long span between learning about God's supernatural gifts and trying to use them.

Although it never occurred to me to ask for the grace to fast, in a special way I believe I received it from Our Lady. That first Friday, it was extremely difficult for my co-workers to understand my reasons for fasting. I was ridiculed almost to the point where I did not think I could take anymore. I was incredibly sensitive. So many times, I was near tears and had all I could do to hold them back. But after a few weeks, they knew that I was serious and, amazingly, they supported me. That was a grace!

It was similar with friends. For years I would get together with girlfriends that I grew up with. We'd go to dinner to celebrate one another's birthdays. Traditionally, this would be on a Friday. I knew the girls felt uncomfortable eating in front of me. It was not easy for them, and I know it was awkward for me. I often thought, "I would just love to taste that veal cutlet dinner that Seraphine is eating." It was easier with the people at work because it was only for an hour or two at lunch. My friends were blessed with the ability to make dinner stretch to what felt like an eternity. Eventually, I learned how to make a "meal" last for hours, eating my breadsticks very slowly. The girls knew my reason for fasting, likewise my friends at work. It was made more difficult because none of them had heard of Medjugorje. They politely listened when I shared what I was learning, but, in reality, they couldn't have cared less.

Many people who knew me in those years can attest to my weakness in making commitments. Discipline was never a strong trait. Without realizing it, Divine Assistance kept me faithful to fasting. Perhaps in the beginning my ego would not permit me to be swayed, but soon it was more than that. I hoped to help Chucky through my vow of fasting. I had headaches in the beginning, yet I went on marathon fasts for thirty-six hours without even bread and water thinking it would be more beneficial to Chucky. My children would warn one another not to bother mommy on Fridays because "she's in a bad mood." I knew that was not what God wanted. I truly had to work at this.

Through the grace of God, I worked through the problems, but it did not happen overnight. It was not until a year later that I gained some insights into fasting. I learned that Jesus was the Bread of Life. Bread was essential then for more than just its physical nutrients. I realized I needed spiritual direction to help me gain a higher degree of closeness with God, a degree that God has planned for me and that I might attain through prayer and fasting. This spiritual direction could have come from a deacon, a religious Sister or a Priest, or even a lay person who was close to God. My reluctance to communicate with religious in general hampered me.

I did not understand why prayer and fasting were vital together. I was once told that one can't fast without prayer. I pretended I knew that, but it was really the first time I had given it any thought. In reading Our Lady's messages, "fast" and "pray" are always linked because each makes the other possible. As I meet people now who are learning about Medjugorje and trying to live the messages, I rejoice for them. They can share with a community of others about the problems of fasting. My promise to Our Lady to fast on bread and water was on hearsay, as only a handful of people reflected seriously on or even knew of Our Lady's urgent message for peace. The grace of trusting God to feed me as I hungered to know Him better and to love Him more came through fasting. Our Lady was teaching me, via these six children, and bringing me closer to Her Son.

As I prayed to the Blessed Mother while saying that one decade, I longed to know more about the lives of Jesus and Mary. I learned the mysteries of the rosary in grade school, but I had long since forgotten them. So, I borrowed my daughter's fifth grade prayer book and looked for explanations. Through the precious gift of this book, I became aware of the life, death, and resurrection of Jesus. My knowledge of Christ was enhanced, and my desire to know Him better was becoming real.

Throughout the next few months, I longed for conversations with others who could challenge me spiritually. Our Lady knew and answered my needs. A neighbor of eight years suddenly began to share her favorite scripture verses with me. Before a family vacation, she offered her daughter's Bible in case I had some quiet time for reading. She did not give me any direction where to start. I simply knew I had the Good News in my hands. I treasured it. I can't help but smile as I recall the year prior to my reawakening and asking Janet, "What is the difference between the New Testament and the Old Testament?" Ironically, instead of reading a novel at the pool on our vacation, I was captivated by parables that Jesus used as He taught.

My neighbor very gently talked about a special peace she received through prayer. As she spoke of the Holy Spirit, I wondered with embarrassment who that was. I had equated the Holy Spirit with a dove. I do not brag of my ignorance, and yet, it is important to be shared.

A beautiful chain of events led me to many people that summer of '83, whose spirituality became etched in my heart. One conversation which I truly feel Our Lord arranged will always stand out in my mind. A friend was telling me about a prayer group she'd belonged to when she lived in upstate New York. She told me how the power of the Holy Spirit filled this group, particularly when they prayed over her by what she called, "Laying Hands." She shared that she was blessed with a peace which assured her that, no matter what happened in her life, God was present. I envied that feeling. She mentioned a prayer group on Long Island which she had heard was very gifted. They met weekly at nearby

Molloy College. At the time, I was leery of these new terms: prayer groups, Holy Spirit, and Laying Hands. This was not for me.

Denis Dillon's name was mentioned as one of the leaders of the prayer group at Molloy College. I was intrigued by the fact that he belonged to a prayer group. I'd been hoping to meet Denis Dillon someday. It was his talk on the reported apparitions in Medjugorje that initially spurred me to seek Mary's help and at the same time to discover her motherly love.

I continued praying the rosary and read about the fifteen promises that Our Lady made to St. Dominic and Blessed Alan in the 13th century to those who recite the rosary. One of the promises was, "I have obtained from my Divine Son that all the advocates of the rosary shall have for intercessors the entire celestial court during their life and at the hour of death."

All this took place in three summer months, and afterwards I began to pray the rosary in full. In August, I was given a book about a priest named Padre Pio, of whom I had never heard. Padre Pio was a Capuchin Friar, known by his fellow friars as a man who conversed with Jesus, the saints and angels, and who for the last fifty years of his life bore in his own flesh the wounds of Christ. As I continued to read Padre Pio's biography, I was amazed to learn that even after his death in 1968, his spirit was present to many. The book described what is called an "Odor of Sanctity." Some say it is like an overwhelming fragrance of a perfume. As I read the testimonies of those who claimed miraculous healings through the intercession of Padre Pio, my room suddenly filled with the fragrance of an indescribable perfume. At first, I said, "No way, this couldn't be." The fragrance grew stronger and stronger. Instead of saying, "No way," I should have been saying, "Thank you," and so I did. I prayed through the intercession of Padre Pio to learn to love and serve God as he did, so that I might allow God to fulfill the purpose for my existence. Padre Pio's imitation of Christ was my example. I prayed to be his Spiritual Child and the "Odor of Sanctity" that filled my room that night was my confirmation that my prayers were answered. Praying to Padre Pio, whom I felt was among the celestial court in Heaven, united me more closely to the rosary.

During that summer, still in my infancy stage of prayer, Karen and John would call from their home in Pennsylvania. Our three-way conversations were the spiritual nourishment and support each of us needed. Karen was our rock. Before David was born, John had surrendered his academic knowledge of God's love. Now John was striving to allow God to speak to him through his heart. Through David, John and I shared the same timing. We were both taking baby steps to God, saying, "This child is yours. Show us your love through him."

That September of 1983, Karen and John invited me to join them at a Charismatic Rally at Nassau Coliseum, an indoor stadium on Long Island. I wasn't sure what to expect. Being aware that the theme was the power of the Holy Spirit, I knew it was finally time to learn, "Who is the Holy Spirit?"

I was excited to be among twelve hundred men and women to spend the entire day at this conference. I was unaccustomed to the phrase, "Charismatic." People praised God with their raised arms and sang with a strength and fervor I had never witnessed before. Then suddenly, a hush would come over the crowd. If I close my eyes, I can still recall the harmonious blend of gentle song that whispered in foreign tongues. According to Webster's definition of the gift of tongues, it is categorized as a divinely granted gift or supernatural ability to speak in a language unknown to the speaker. The dynamic charism of each speaker at this conference impressed in my spirit a new truth I was discovering. God had so much that He wanted to give us through the Third Person of the Blessed Trinity, the Holy Spirit.

David was in my arms for most of the day. He was a little uncomfortable during the Holy Mass. I left my seat so he wouldn't disturb those around us with his slight cries. I found a quiet nook and sat on the steps in full view of the altar. At this time, the Blessed Trinity made their home in my heart. I realized God's love in His gift of this precious child, clothed in struggle, as was Mary's infant, as she held Him in Her arms.

We brought our lunches to the Coliseum that day, as suggested. What I never failed to include was chocolate candy.

The thought came to me that Our Blessed Mother asks us to offer up sacrifices to God, no matter how big or small. I offered my love for chocolate indefinitely to Our Lord for my nephew David. I did not look to make a deal with God. I simply wanted to make a sacrifice in David's name. To offer up all our sacrifices is Mary's message. I wanted to live that message.

One of the speakers at the Charismatic Rally was Father John Bertolucci. He related that our Blessed Mother was reportedly appearing daily to six young children in Yugoslavia. This was the first time I had heard anything mentioned about Medjugorje since May. I literally consumed every word Father was saying. During intermission, a film on the apparitions in Medjugorje would be shown in the lobby.

John and Karen had gone to Fatima at Easter to pray to Our Lady for her intercession for a healing for David. During intermission, John, with David, and I headed for the lobby to see the film. We watched the film with almost a hundred other people. With so many voices around us, we couldn't hear the comments from Fr. Bertolucci, but our eyes were fixed on the screen like glue. Later, all I could remember of the film was seeing the children climb up the mountain where they claimed to have first seen the Blessed Mother. I turned to John and said, "John, that's our next stop."

Chapter Three

Making a Journey

March 2, 1984. I could not believe that I was kissing Mike and our children good-bye and really going off to Yugoslavia. I had been half joking when I said to John, "That's our next stop." Who knew Our Lady would be listening?

John telephoned in mid-January to tell me that he was going to take David to Medjugorje. Karen couldn't get time off from her teaching job. David was only eighteen months old, and his needs were so many. How in the world could John drive around in that Communist country all by himself? But there was no doubt in John's mind that he and David were going.

I asked Mike if he would mind if I went with them. Through the grace of God, Mike said, "No problem." I was able to get time off from work, although the ridicule I endured until the day I left was beyond belief. Mike and our children understood, and that was all that mattered.

When we landed at Dubrovnik, a city on the southwest coast of Croatia, we had no idea how to get to Medjugorje. We only knew one person who had ever been there. Other than saying it was near a city called Mostar, he certainly had not been a wealth of information.

We were off to a great start. At the airport, John discovered he had lost his traveler's checks. We planned to call home about the missing checks as soon as we settled into a hotel. Mostar did not seem to be more than an hour away on the map, and after twelve hours of traveling from New York, one more hour didn't seem too much. Three hours later, we finally reached our destination.

Our first experience in this foreign land almost convinced me that we should turn around and go back home. Our rented car would not go into reverse which made driving quite a challenge. As we drove into Mostar, John tried to make a U-turn on a crowded street. Everyone was yelling at us. We were stuck across the lanes as the cars and buses unceasingly honked their horns. I was in the back seat with David when finally a young man came to help. He told John to get out of the driver's seat. When John got out, this fellow jumped into the front seat and took off with David and me in the car. I could not believe what was happening. I will never forget John running down the block after us. It was like something out of a movie. We were taken to this fellow's house, which was only down the road. His intention was to fix the clutch for us. John and I roared with laughter when he shared what was going on in his mind as he ran after us. How would he ever tell Karen and Mike that he lost us in Yugoslavia?

We finally found a hotel that could accommodate us and promised heat in our room. We made ourselves comfortable and waited for the heat to rise, but it never did. The room was like an icicle. The temperatures in Croatia were below freezing, and David's body temperature was extremely delicate. About to collapse from total exhaustion, we were blessed with a gift from Our Lady. John found his traveler's checks.

Early the next morning, we asked for directions to Medjugorje. The hotel management knew of the village but were reluctant to get involved in a conversation about it. The reason might have been the number of soldiers around the hotel. The authorities were not happy with the events happening in Medjugorje. The government saw the faith of the people who were streaming to this little village as a threat to them.

When we asked others for directions, we had no idea what they were saying. The Serbo-Croatian language is very different from English. Thank God for their arm waving. We left Mostar with vague instructions on how to get there. It seemed like they had told us that Medjugorje was down the block. What a joke that turned out to be! Medjugorje turned out to be in the opposite direction from where we had been told. "Down the block" was up a mountain and forty-five minutes away.

Only by a newspaper article in the Philadelphia Standard Times, which was sent to Karen two days before we left, were we able to recognize the church of St. James from the road. As we spotted the two lofty steeples from the photo, my heart pounded with joy. I couldn't believe we were finally there.

The church was half-filled with a group of pilgrims, and a priest was talking to them from the altar in Italian. After they left, John and I prayed a rosary. We offered our thanks together to Our Blessed Lord in insuppressible tears for bringing us to Medjugorje. We had journeyed half-way across the world with this special angel, David, who weighed only thirteen pounds.

Most people had said, "What's the use?" John and I had come to Medjugorje (which means between the mountains) to pray to Our Lady to intercede for a miracle that David desperately needed. I didn't realize my own desperate need. Before leaving New York, my girlfriend, Janet, gifted me with a journal and the words, "May you return with a faith stronger than those mountains." Through my concentration on David, God was about to touch me. It would be me who was healed. My weak faith began to resemble the strength of those mountains as God's mercy, love and compassion be-came our vessel in a sea of grace.

That first day, Our Lady brought us to each person she wanted us to meet. Shortly after leaving the church, John and I saw the priest who had been on the altar. We approached him and gave him a letter that Karen had written in Italian. She was hoping one of the visionaries could ask Our Lady for prayers for David. Father read the letter, and, in broken

English, he asked us to pray for God's will to be done. Then he invited us into the room where Our Lady would be with the visionary children that evening. We could not believe it. It all seemed like a dream.

Father pointed out the path to the small mountain, Podbrodo, where Our Lady first appeared. John and I carried David up the mountain, taking advantage of the jagged rocks for footholds. We brushed against thorn bushes throughout our climb. It took us five decades of the rosary and what seemed like an eternity to reach the top. We were finally standing where Our Lady first appeared. There was no need or desire for words. We stood and prayed.

As we were about to descend the mountain, an old Croatian woman smiled at us and held her arms out for the baby. I did not know what she wanted to do with David, but I entrusted him to her. Before we knew it, she began to carry David down the mountain – like she had wings on her feet! At the bottom of the hill, the woman put David in my arms and her rosary beads around his neck. A young man from the village translated that the old lady wanted us to come to her house for coffee. But it was getting late and time to get back to church. We declined and said thank you the best way we could. We hoped we would see her again.

Father told John and I that the Mass began at 6 p.m. He said they begin to pray the rosary at 5 and, if we could be there a little early, we should go straight into the apparition room. I did not feel comfortable walking into the church, bypassing everyone who was in the aisles, to go into this special room that is to the right of the altar. I motioned to John that we should pray in the pew before going any further. We were not kneeling more than a minute when a nun at the opposite end of the pew came over to us. I was amazed that she spoke English. She introduced herself as Sister Janja and said, "You must be the Americans that Fr. Slavko told me about." When we told her we were from New York, she beamed. Sister told us she had been assigned to New York for six years and recently returned home to visit her family. At that time, she was asked to assist in Medjugorje and was living in the convent there.

Sister told us there would be an English-speaking priest in church that evening and asked if we would like him to hear our confessions. Normally, I get very up-tight when it's time to go to confession. But without realizing it, something very special happened within me. I was glad to be given the chance to go to confession, and I prayed to make it my best. When we say "yes," Our Lady takes care of all the details. The hope of speaking to another person in English was like a dream. As inconceivable as it seemed, Our Lady was using Sister as a link to bring us closer to Our Lord through the Sacrament of Reconciliation. When we entered the apparition room, an aura of tranquility brought us to our knees.

The room in which we prayed with David was utter simplicity. My knees were glued to the cold tiled floor as I knelt in front of a magnificent old statue of Our Lady. The statue was in a corner, to the right of a table. This table was about three feet away from the wall, with a very simple crucifix fixed above it. Many people came into the room bringing rosaries, candles, bottles of water, and other articles. They left them on this table. It was behind this table that Our Lady reportedly appeared. These objects would receive a special blessing. I put the picture of David taken when he was just born on the table.

A local English-speaking priest came into the room and introduced himself as Fr. Svetozar Kraljevic. He too, along with Sr. Janja, had been assigned in New York at the Croatian Church of Saints Cyril and Methodius on West 41st and 10th Ave. This room adjacent to the main altar was now filled with men, women, and children kneeling shoulder to shoulder praying the rosary in unison with the congregation in the main church.

After the Sorrowful Mysteries of the rosary were recited, the children who see Our Lady came into the room. Jakov, Marija, Vicka, and Ivan stood in front of the table, blessed themselves and began to pray. There were no halos on their heads. They were ordinary children in every way. As they prayed, all four fell down to their knees at the exact same moment. We could see that they were riveted on one spot. They would nod their heads as if responding in conversation. Vicka broke into a smile that extended from ear to ear. I wondered what Our Lady could be saying.

I didn't concentrate on the visionaries, for I was holding David and praying to Our Lady. I believed from deep within that the Blessed Mother was in the room with us. There was so much I wanted to say, but to simply give her all of my anxieties at that moment was what was placed in my heart.

The time from when the children knelt down to when they all looked up at the same moment and gasped, "Ode," (which means, "She is gone") was only about sixty seconds. Immediately after the apparition, the children knelt down behind the main altar with a priest and led the congregation in prayer that was followed by a Mass. Sr. Janja suggested we stay in the apparition room during Mass. With David so motionless in my arms, I wondered over and over in my mind: "Mother Mary, are you still here with us?"

We remained in the room and prayed for a while after Mass. This little room was ice cold because there was no heat in the church, but the warmth that radiated from Our Lady's presence during her appearance and the presence of Our Lord in the tabernacle to the left of the room was incredible. The peace of Jesus and Mary furnished us with a blanket of love that we relished. We were not anxious to leave the room at all. Without our asking, three of the priests from the main altar came into the room and laid their hands on John who sat with David on his lap. I knelt down on John's right side and placed my hands on David. The five of us were one as we prayed for this special child. I cannot adequately describe how moved I was by the intensity of their prayers. I had never experienced anything like that before.

Father Svetozar then heard John's confession in the main church and this gave me some time to recollect. Wow! I thought I had been making this journey to help John out with David. Now I was sure that God had plans for me, too. God's work had brought me here, and this realization overwhelmed me. So, I began to search my soul and examine my conscience in preparation for my own confession.

I never would have gone to confession unless it was behind a screen in a dark confessional box. But Our Lady gently prepared me for what I've come to realize. Confession should be face to face with nothing to fear, and so it was. Father and I sat in a pew, and you could hear a pin drop. It was as if the Heavens were listening. Our Lord, through Father, filled my heart and soul with tremendous peace and the security of knowing how much God loved me through the priceless gift of reconciliation.

On the plane en route to Medjugorje, I had written in my journal "March 2, 1984: And if, Sweet Lord, you do not have it in your plans to heal David yet, I know it's for the best reasons and we will not question, for Thy Will, not ours, be done." I prayed that God would help me say this and really mean it, no matter how much it hurt. "My view is so narrow, while Yours is all-encompassing. My will is merely human, Yours is perfect wisdom. My thoughts are for the present, and your plan, Heavenly Father, is for all eternity."

At the end of my confession, Father asked me to accept God's will in accepting David just as he was. Our Lady was teaching me how to pray through David, just as he was. If David were "a perfect child," certainly, I would not have been there. When Chucky died, I knew that I needed to pray more than at any other time in my life. I believed that I was praying for Chucky. In Medjugorje, with David clothed in struggle, I was searching for a cure for David. I realize now that Our Lady was teaching me how to pray so that I could find peace within my own heart and with God. Our Lady gently changed my path and took me by the hand as we walked together more easily and with greater security towards Her Son.

I had a lot of work to do. So, when Father asked, "Will you help spread Our Lady's message when you get back to the states?" My response was an immediate "Yes."

On our second day in Medjugorje, it seemed as if we wouldn't need a car to drive up the mountain from Mostar. Our spirits were so high, I think we could have flown. Driving into the village, we went straight to St. James and prayed a rosary. Nearing the fourth decade, our tears of thanksgiving seemed to be in consonance with David's slight smile.

Then, we found the young man that we had met the day before at the bottom of the Hill of Apparition. John and I hoped he could direct us to the woman's house who had carried David down the mountain. We wanted to thank her once again. We knocked on the door of the house, but no one knew of her. As we were about to abandon our quest, a man who spoke German came to our aid. His warmth and caring was overwhelming. John and I were perfect strangers, yet he invited us into his neighbor's house, a man named Marinko.

Marinko and his wife, Dragica, insisted that we have some coffee. Dragica fell in love with David immediately. What we thought would be a very short visit, turned out to be one of the greatest unexpected gifts in our lives. As the family spoke with John in German, I began to feel a little left out. But the love they demonstrated for David as they touched and tenderly helped him became my means of communication. Then came a grace beyond belief.

Marinko's son, who was about thirteen years of age, put a videotape in the V.C.R. I was surprised that they even had a television in this remote hamlet. The tape that began to play brought a smile to my face. It was in English. Six months prior, John and I had been straining to hear the voice of the commentator of the film at the Coliseum on Long Island. Here, Fr. Bertolucci was on the screen and, ironically, John and I could hear his every word in a family room in Medjugorje.

Father spoke of the children who see Our Lady. The German-speaking man said that one of the girls, Vicka, lived next door and two of the other children, Marija and Jakov, lived down the road. We never imagined we would be meeting the visionaries personally, but praise God, Our Lady had other plans. Marinko called on the telephone and, about ten minutes later, Vicka, Marija, and Jakov walked in. My first thought was, "How lucky they are that they see Our Lady." The ordinary mannerisms of the children impressed me the most. Vicka held David for almost a half hour, and I wondered if she was speaking to Our Lady in her heart, for her face was glowing. When Marija cradled David, her serenity shone. Jakov reminded me of my son, Michael - shy in front of strangers, but with Marinko's family, Marija and Vicka, united in love and harmony. Later, I saw Jakov outside shooting a basketball in a hoop with his friends. I realized then that they were no different from most children except they see Our Lady.

John asked in his high school German if it would be possible for the children to ask Our Blessed Mother a question. Immediately, Vicka agreed. If we wrote it down, Sr. Janja would be able to translate it and either Jakov or Ivan would ask the question. John wrote, "Will Jesus heal David?" I asked John if he would ask a question about Chucky. On the same slip of paper he wrote, "If Chucky is in Purgatory, how can I help lift him up to Heaven?" I had no intention of asking Our Blessed Mother what I could to do to relieve the burden buried deeply within my own heart. How well Our Mother knows us. We can hide nothing from her. Our Lady knew that simply by asking this question the weight from my heart would be lifted.

Sister Janja had welcomed John and me in the apparition room each night that we were in Medjugorje. She said it would be more convenient for taking care of David. Changing and feeding him during the three hours that we were in church was much easier in this small grace-filled room. What a blessing this invitation was! In just a few moments, Our Lady would speak to us through the children.

I was so nervous. Just before the children came into the room, I reached for my picture of David and put it on the table. Ivan walked into the room followed by Marija, Vicka, and Jakov. Their smiles dissipated all my anxieties. All my confidence in Our Lady's intercession returned, stronger than ever. A Franciscan friar gave Ivan our questions. As they began praying, they simultaneously fell to their knees. For John and me, the following moments were emotion-filled. I kept wondering if Ivan would ask Our Lady about David. We were behind the children, and the room was crowded. All we could do was pray with all our hearts and be prepared to surrender ourselves to the will of God.

As they sighed, "Ode," they blessed themselves. Ivan stood up and went over to the table and picked up David's picture. He gave Sr. Janja the picture, and they spoke briefly. The answer would be ours in a moment. Oh, how I prayed for patience. Sister turned to us and said, "Mary gives you hope. Fast on Wednesdays and Fridays and pray seven Our Fathers, seven Hail Marys and seven Glory Be's, and the Apostle's creed every day, and pray more daily." An answer from the Mother of God! I'll never forget Sister saying, "Mary gives you hope!"

We cried with joy. The excitement of hearing Our Lady's words filled the ensuing moments of silence with countless unspoken words. Our hearts were bursting with love and thanksgiving. I could not have hugged David any tighter. A peace I have never known before filled my heart with gladness as David slept so still in my arms. I said to John, "I know that answer was for both of our questions and, from that moment on, my prayers and fasting on Wednesdays and Fridays will go for David, because he is living, and he really needs our prayers." John, having never met Chucky, turned to me and said, "I will offer up my prayers and sacrifices for Chucky, too." As I helped David, he knew he was to help Chucky. My mom and dad and brother and sisters couldn't understand my desire to fast, and Our Lady knew my loneliness. I was now blessed to be able to share prayer and fasting with John.

We went back to the hotel and called Karen. "Mary gives us hope. We are to fast and to pray." As a joke, we added, "Tomorrow is Wednesday, don't eat." Karen laughed, "Good thing I had already planned on fasting." When we said our prayers that night, we wondered if the seven Our Fathers, seven Hail Marys and seven Glory Be's could be included in the rosary, or should they be extra prayers? Our Lady must have been smiling at us. We get an answer from the Mother of God, and we were already trying to bargain!

Our next two days in Medjugorje were filled with innumerable graces. As Father Vlasic, the spiritual director of the seers, unexpectedly came into the apparition room after Mass and prayed over David, I felt that was a special gift that God reserved for us. No one else was in the room. Had Our Lady brought Father through that door? As Father prayed over John who held David in his arms, I prayed in front of the statue of Our Lady in the corner of the room. The only words that I was able to utter silently and continuously were "Jesus, have mercy. Jesus, have mercy." I emptied myself in that prayer. Before I knew it, my whole body was shaking, and I could not stop. The spirit of Father's prayers was intense, and he prayed for a long time. My trembling stopped at the exact time Father's prayers ended. The calm that came over me was complete.

Driving down the mountain to Mostar that evening, I said to John, "I know something special happened in that room tonight." I wasn't sure in what way, but I knew that Father's prayers had created a joy in me that was like a bubble about to burst. I was so excited that I could not understand why John did not feel what I felt.

As I prayed the following morning for the best words to describe what I had experienced in the apparition room, I opened my Bible to the Gospel of St. John, 9:39, *"I came into this world for judgment, so that those who do not see might see, and those who do see might become blind."* No doctor would ever confirm that my sight was restored from blindness, but through the intercession of Our Lady in Medjugorje, Our Divine Healer healed me of spiritual blindness.

John and I spent our last night in Dubrovnik, alongside the Adriatic Sea. John stayed with David in the room of our hotel, and I went for a walk along the coast. I reflected on all the blessings we had received during our trip and on the heavenly protection we had been graced with. My instinctive way of saying "thank you" to Jesus for sending his Mother to our aid here on earth was by clapping my hands. I thought I was all alone, but, tucked away in the shadows about fifty yards from me was a couple admiring the moonlight. They must have thought I was out of my mind, but nothing phased me. I could have stood on top of the world and said, "Thank you, Mary, you are truly Queen of Heaven and Earth and Queen of my heart, and I LOVE YOU!"

Mary's message of prayer, fasting, reconciliation, faith and conversion was budding in me through the gift of bringing David to Medjugorje. I asked the blessed Mother to take my hand and never let it go so that she would always be my guide. I was on the road to discovering the true love of God. And with Our Lady's ever-patient direction, I rejoiced in realizing there was no turning back!

Chapter Four

No Turning Back

"If I speak in human and angelic tongues but do not have love, I am a resounding gong or a clashing cymbal." (1 Cor 13:1)

In the summer of 1983, before my trip to Medjugorje, I was still so new to prayer. Many times, I became frustrated, searching for the right words to say. During this time, I received a precious gift. I knelt in church praying to the Blessed Mother. I sincerely asked Our Lady in front of the Blessed Sacrament to teach me how to pray and how to love. David's mother, Karen, sat next to me as we waited for a Nuptial Mass to begin. She handed me an envelope. I read it slowly, the words melting in my heart. It was exactly what I had tried to say to Our Lady just moments before. It has become my favorite prayer to Our Lady.

"Dear Mother Mary,
Open your arms and receive your child,
Be mine in joy; we shall laugh together.
Be mine in sorrow; your touch will lighten my pain.

Be mine in his hectic pace of living; your serenity will
restore my peace.

Be mine in the stillness when I cannot sense God's
presence;

Your loving example will be my guide.

Dear Mother Mary, be my teacher. Help me to still the
clamor of the many voices around me and listen only
to God's Holy Spirit.

Oh, Mother Mary, help me when my spirit fails to turn
to your Son with trust and love.

A mother knows her child. You know me.

A mother helps her child. You've helped me.

A mother loves her child. I know that you love me.

Be with me, dear Mother Mary, and we shall be one in
love, our hearts part of the divine circle of love, with
your Son, Our Lord, Jesus Christ."

With Our Lady as my teacher, I conscientiously pledged
to try never to disappoint her. I had so much to be thankful
for. It was now time to stop being selfish in keeping the gifts
that God had given me through His Mother. I wanted to give
a little something of myself to say thank you to Jesus and to
Mary.

On December 31, 1983, I telephoned my best friend,
Janet, to wish her and her family a very Happy New Year.
Without planning to do so, I asked Janet if she wanted to
volunteer with me to work in the cancer care unit of Mercy

Hospital. Mercy is located near our home and is the only one of its kind where we live in Nassau County, NY. I learned of the volunteer program only two months before when God, who is so very gentle and subtle, planted a seed in my heart by another friend who volunteered how rewarding it was for her to be with and comfort those who are sick and near death. She said that it was difficult at times, but that the six weeks of preparatory instructions, one night a week, would prepare me. So, when I mentioned this to Janet, she agreed immediately.

Although I honestly thought I was ready, I was quite frightened. I had always avoided going to a hospital, even to visit someone. I'm squeamish when it comes to sights and smells. For the life of me, I couldn't understand how I would be doing this. It had to be God! Janet and I volunteered for Thursday evenings. Each time we volunteered, the two of us found quiet time in which to share our experiences with different patients or families by whom we were touched. *"There is an appointed time for everything, and a time for every affair under the heavens. He had made everything appropriate to its time."* (Eccl 3: 1 & 11)

I did a lot of mechanical chores: going for linens, filling up pitchers of water, emptying garbage, running to the pharmacy. I volunteered for those jobs to avoid getting too close to the patients. One night, I went into one room to refill the ice water and did a double take. I didn't even know if the completely bald patient was a man or a woman. I have to admit, it really upset me. After a couple of weeks, I felt comfortable going into the rooms, but only if the patients were asleep. Once they were asleep, I took a deep breath and gave a sigh of relief. I wondered, if I felt this uncomfortable, was I really supposed to be here?

In the third week working on the unit, I was asked to sit with a beautiful elderly woman named Elizabeth. She was very confused because of the medication and simply needed someone to talk to. I became much more relaxed. To sit and talk or even to listen to someone talk, was prayer. Very slowly, the defensive manner I'd adopted began to disappear. I had always had a soft spot for the aged and infirm. But probably after Chucky died, I'd built up a tremendous wall against the pain of separation. Through the grace of Our Lady, God very gently pruned away those defenses and allowed me to feel again.

On a particular drive to the hospital after the first month, while praying the rosary, I suddenly realized that I was doing this work because of Our Lady and her example of compassion. How often must Mary have said in her heart: *"My Son, my Son. If only I had died instead of you. My son, my son."* (2 Sm 19:1) The rosary was the link that not only introduced us, but also brought us closer every day. I never "felt" Our Lady's presence as so many people claim, but deep inside, I was blessed with an immense awareness of her love for me. I felt that Our Blessed Mother had asked Jesus for extra graces for me because I was trying so hard to love Him more.

I knew that day that I never wanted to let go of Our Lady. I felt as Peter did as he was walking on the water. When he took his eyes off Christ, who was also on the water, he began to drown. (Mt 14:28-33)

As part of my morning prayers to Our Lord, I began to ask for help to have the practical wisdom to look to His Mother every step of the way. My volunteering in a cancer care unit was through Our Lady, my new duty to God.

Working as a volunteer is terrific because, although you're there to help the nurses, they make no demands on you. The nurses are tuned into and aware of which volunteer is best for which job. If a nurse needed an aide to stand by as she changed a tracheotomy, Janet would be right in that room without a second thought. A nurse who needed a volunteer to sit with a patient chose me. I discovered through the extraordinary gentleness of the nurses how vital it was to have physical contact with the patients. To stroke a patient's forehead, or rub it down with a cool facecloth, or just to hold a hand was, often, the best medicine. To witness the nurses who, in my opinion, are hand-picked by God, care for a patient even after that patient has expired is remarkable. They gently lay hands on the patient as before. They comb their hair and tenderly converse with them with ease. Their sentiments stay with them way beyond the patient's last breath.

Three or four volunteers worked on the unit most nights. Watching the other volunteers was my greatest opportunity to learn how to love. To see Marion, a seasoned volunteer, massage a patient's aching back with such loving care, being extra careful of radiation burns, helped me as I gave my first backrub a week later. To be with Janet in the room in which the patient is semiconscious and watch Janet talk to the patient as if there is a two-way conversation challenged me to do the same. I've always been too embarrassed to talk to someone who can't respond. Yet, I learned how important that was. Patients need to hear those voices, whether they can respond or not.

Standing alongside a patient's bed with another volunteer, Karen, was truly a teaching experience in itself, and a grace. Her laughter and wit, her understanding and sensitivity, all contributed to her impeccable timing.

There was a bond growing between us that Our Lord had knitted together. With all the gifts Our Blessed Lord has bestowed upon us, undeniably the greatest of these is love. (1 Cor. 13:13) *"So faith, hope, love remain, these three; but the greatest of these is love."*

So many times, when a patient on the unit slept, a family member would stay throughout the night. It is such a gift for me to be able to offer that person a cup of coffee and an ear for listening. It's a perfect chance to help that husband, wife, son, or daughter to share what's in his or her heart. Whether it's baseball, the stock market, or death and dying, I thank

God for placing me there. I often wonder if I hadn't lost somebody so close to me, could I possibly feel what they're feeling.

The first time I witnessed about the love of God - I was in the kitchen area of the hospice, rinsing the dinner dishes. A very well-dressed man in his mid-thirties wandered around aimlessly. He'd sit at the table with a cigarette, and then stand by the window. This went on for half an hour. It's hard sometimes to judge if a person wants to be approached. Many simply want to be left alone.

For some reason, I felt his pain, and my heart reached out to him. I offered him a cold drink. We spoke for over an hour. His brother, his identical twin, who was also his best friend, was dying. This young man was literally dying with his brother, of a broken heart. He shared their childhood days with me. He spoke of his brother's illness and of his not being able to cope. His brother was at peace with dying, but he wasn't. Everything was going wrong for him. Not only was he losing his brother but, as he spoke, he reminded me of the story of Job. Job was a good man who suffered total disaster and *"Finally Job broke the silence and cursed the day on which he had been born."* (Job 3:1)

The brother of the dying man began to ask: "Why is God allowing this to happen? What is He trying to prove? Is there a God?" A saddened but peaceful spirit brought me back to 1983 when it was I who asked those questions.

It was Holy Thursday night and, before working, I had stopped in the chapel for a visit. As I was leaving, I picked up two pamphlets entitled, "Someone Does Care." Inside was a picture in a green light of the upper torso of Christ on the cross with the quote, *"In this we have known the charity of God because he hath laid down His life for us."* (1 Jn 3:16) Opposite the picture was written, "Did you ever study a picture of an image of your suffering Savior?" The pamphlet read:

"Study the touching picture of the dying Christ on this folder. Note the weary, aching, thorn-crowned Head; the sacred Face defiled with spittle; the parched Lips; the pierced Hands; the bruised and bleeding Body. As you make this simple meditation, you will recall that He, the sinless One, the God-Man, suffered and died for you.

"When your crosses seem to crush your aching heart; when you feel discouraged and become erroneously convinced that no one cares, just pause for a moment and study the suffering Christ.

"You will feel a new strength within you, become more encouraged, and bear your crosses more patiently because you will be convinced that someone does care, more than you shall ever know."

Our Lord's timing was flawless. I handed the dying man's brother this small leaflet. He quietly read it and was noticeably moved by it. There was no need for further words. I'm not sure if we will ever see each other again as I don't even know his name. I never even met his brother because, as I called on Good Friday to inquire of the nurses how his brother was doing, I was told that he died that morning.

God revealed Himself to me that night. That man whom God placed in my life for that one hour was Christ Himself. I thought I was helping a very sad man let go of his brother, but God was there in his place helping me to let go of my brother. I understand now why I was awake until 2 a.m. that morning. I had been struggling not only with someone else's problem, but with my own problem, with the inevitability of dying. A beautiful thought entered my mind, and I'm sure Our Lady planted it. "Let go and let God - He's not going to leave you alone."

In volunteering, I receive so much more than I could possibly give because Our Lady helps me to see Jesus in others. I was walking past a room on the unit one day and heard a very weak voice practically whisper: "Water, Water!" As I was giving this patient water, I was suddenly overwhelmed with the thought that it was Christ who whispered, "Water, water!" *"For I was hungry and you gave me food, I was thirsty and you gave me drink, a stranger and you welcomed me, naked and you clothed me, ill and you cared for me, in prison and you visited me." Then the righteous will answer him and say, 'Lord, when did we see you hungry and feed you, or thirsty and give you drink? When did we see you a stranger and welcome you, or naked and clothe you? When did we see you ill or in prison, and visit you?' And the king will say to them in reply, 'Amen, I say to you, whatever you did for one of these least brothers of mine, you did for me."* (Mt 25:35) I thank you Lord for whispering, "Water, water," and giving me this chance to serve you.

Our Lady in Medjugorje gave this message to the visionaries on August 28, 1986, **"Dear Children! My call is that in everything you would be an image for others, especially in prayer and witnessing. Dear children, without you I am not able to help the world. I desire that you cooperate with me in everything, even in the smallest things. Therefore, dear children, help me by letting your prayer be from the heart and all of you surrendering completely to me. That way I shall be able to teach and lead you on this way which I have begun with you. Thank you for having responded to my call."**

When I read this message, I was really touched by the phrase, "Help Me." It took quite a while to truly understand that the Mother of God needs us to help her. Working in the hospital has taught me that the smallest task such as emptying a garbage can be a means of witnessing and can bear fruit. A friend of mine was visiting a patient on the unit. I tried to move quickly as I changed the refuse in the adjoining room so as not to disturb their visit, but my friend asked me to share Our Lady's message from Medjugorje with the woman she was visiting. Our Lord was creating the opportunity to witness. All I had to do was say, "Yes." One of Our Lady's first messages to the visionaries in 1981 was, "I have come to tell you that God exists!" We spoke briefly of how blessed we were to know that God exists. I was able to share, that a few years prior, God was merely an occasional thought to me. Most times, witnessing is most effective in the simplest ways.

Many conversations are initiated because of a pin I wear of Our Lady, which is a visible means of witnessing. When someone comments on my pin, I beam. It's so special when a patient shares his or her love for Our Lady. One man referred to himself as a "Hail Mary Man," all of his life. He believes that the million Hail Marys he said during the Korean War was what brought him home safely.

Our Lady's message to the children in Medjugorje on August 8, 1985, was, **"Dear Children! Today I call you especially now to advance against Satan by means of prayer. Satan wants to work still more now that you know he is at work. Dear children, put on the armor for battle and with the rosary in your hand defeat him! Thank you for having responded to my call."**

I take Our Lady's messages literally. I believe in that armor. If it's feasible, most times I have my rosary in my hand. One night in the hospital, I kept company with a patient named Mr. Jones who was unable to talk because of a recent tracheotomy. He was restless and couldn't sleep.

After we had finished about five games of tic-tac-toe, I asked him if he would like me to look through a magazine with him. He had a magazine on his night table that I had never seen. It was obviously geared to the tastes of the wealthy. I was in awe thumbing through it. Here and there, he would point out exorbitantly priced gun collections. Deep inside, my heart ached for him. I thought: "Here this man has probably less than six months to live, and these are his priorities?" It made me feel so sad.

As I was turning the pages in the magazine, Mr. Jones noticed my rosary and motioned to see it. I asked if he would like a rosary of his own, and he nodded affirmatively. He took the rosary, but later tossed it aside. I was hurt by this, but I prayed not to reveal my emotions. We continued looking at the magazine. As I was getting ready to leave, he reached for the rosary and began to caress the crucifix.

The following week, when his wife was visiting, I stopped in to say hello. The rosary was tied to the side of his bed. I felt a special glow inside as I saw it there. I was in the kitchen area the following Thursday, and Mrs. Jones was sitting among a group of people. She asked me if I was the one who had given her husband the rosary. She introduced me to her husband's family. His brother and his brother's wife were at the table. They said I looked familiar and suddenly realized why. Three months prior, I had been in New Jersey sharing about Our Lady's messages. They were there that evening. His brother asked me about David and said that is how he remembered me. God's timing was superb. Three months ago in New Jersey, and now this night in which his brother was so close to death, we were sharing about the Mother of God. The rosary that his brother had next to his bed was blessed in Medjugorje. During the week, Mr. Jones was called home by God. I felt strongly convinced that Our Lady was right there to bring him to Her Son.

Our Lady's message of November 14, 1985, comes to my mind so often. **"Dear Children! I, your Mother, love you and wish to urge you to prayer. I am tireless, dear children, and I am calling you even then, when you are far away from my heart. I am a Mother, and even though I feel pain for each one who goes astray, I forgive easily and am happy for every child who returns to me. Thank you for having responded to my call."**

"Is a lamp brought in to be placed under a bushel basket or under a bed, and not to be placed on a lampstand? For there is nothing hidden except to be made visible; nothing is secret except to come to light. Anyone who has ears to hear ought to hear," He also told them, *"Take care what you hear. The measure with which you measure will be measured out to you, and still more will be given to you. To the one who has, more will be given; from the one who has not, even what he has will be taken away."*

I had been given so many graces from God through the Blessed Mother. I know that I am not to hide these graces as one does not *"light a lamp and then put it under a basket; it*

is set on a lampstand, where it gives light to all in the house."
(Mt 5:15) My love, respect, admiration, reverence and near-
ness to Our Lady placed a dependence in her intercession
beyond words. I trust in these following words from the
Catechism of the Catholic Church, paragraphs 967-970: *"By
her complete adherence to the Father's will to his Son's
redemptive work, and to every prompting of the Holy Spirit,
the Virgin Mary is the Church's model of faith and charity.
Thus she is a "preeminent and...wholly unique member of
the Church"; indeed, she is the "exemplary realization" of
the Church.*

*Her role in relation to the Church and to all humanity
goes still further. "In a wholly singularly way she cooperated by her obedience, faith, hope, and burning charity
in the Savior's work of restoring supernatural life to souls.
For this reason she is a mother to us in the order of grace."*

Our Lady has said, **"Dear Children! You are not conscious of the messages which God is sending you through
me. He is giving you great graces and you do not comprehend them. Pray to the Holy Spirit for enlightenment.
If you only knew how great are the graces God is granting
you, you would be praying without ceasing. Thank you for
having responded to my call."** (November 8, 1984.)

St Teresa of Avila said, "For it is one grace to receive the
Lord's favor, another to understand which favor and grace it
is, and a third to know how to describe it."

I fail to find the words to describe all the Lord has done for me, and so I turn to Our Lady for help, for I could never equal her words:

"My soul proclaims the greatness of the Lord;
My spirit rejoices in God my savior.
For he has looked upon his handmaid's lowliness;
Behold, from now on will all will call me blessed
The Mighty One has done great things for me,
And holy is his name."

Chapter Five

Spreading the Message

"Come to me, all you who labor and are burdened, and I will give you rest. Take my yoke upon you and learn from me, for I am meek and humble of heart; and you will find rest for yourselves. For my yoke is easy, and my burden light." (Mt 11:28-30)

Six months before I went to Medjugorje in 1984, I walked into Molloy College out of curiosity to see what a prayer meeting was like. I remember the leader of the meeting asked everyone to take a rock from a pile that he produced. He asked us to place all of our burdens on this rock. After quiet, reflective prayer, he placed the rocks at the foot of the Cross which was in the center of the room. It was a beautiful introduction for me to begin to learn that God wants us to give Him our cares and concerns. After all, He is Our Father, and through His only begotten Son, He begs us to come to Him and He will give us rest.

The man leading the meeting that evening was Denis Dillion, the Nassau County District Attorney. Afterwards, I thanked him for his inspiration. His warm smile and relaxed manner eased the tension I felt and must have projected as I

pre-empted my previous talk. Denis came to me in the chapel and asked if I would be able to share about my trip with David to Medjugorje after Mass. "Oh, Denis, how could you do this to me?" That was what I thought, not what I said. Thank God, I had tucked my notes in my Bible as I left my house. My eight-year-old daughter, Donna, who happened to come to Mass with me that evening, was my stronghold. I looked her way as I spoke. I knew she was proud of me. I prayed Our Lady was proud also.

The following month, when I was asked to speak at a prayer meeting on my own, I panicked and asked Denis if he would come with me and give his talk first. He came and brought a friend, briefly introducing us. The following week, after the meeting at Molloy College, I saw Denis' friend having a cup of coffee. After I had re-introduced myself, he told me that he thought my talk had been very moving, but that I should try to be less glued to my notes. He shared that he had many years tied up in investigating apparitions. He gave me some pointers that I recall instantly even now. I'll never forget his warning: "Kid, it's a lonely world in apparitions. Everybody is going to think you're nuts. You'll find yourself so alone sometimes; you'll even feel as if you're deserted by the heavens. But don't give up on what you believe." We talked at length, and what I learned that evening was merely the beginning of many invaluable teachings from Harry Daley, who became a dear friend who was always there for my innumerable questions.

He was right! Two weeks after I was told that "...it's a lonely world in apparitions," it seemed as if I were on a deserted island. The few people that I had been close to and shared about Medjugorje suddenly believed a rumor that the visionaries were putting on an act, pretending to see Our Lady. They felt this rumor came from a reliable source. My conviction could not change their minds. I remember how I took it personally. Not only did I feel rejected, but I was hurt deep inside for Our Lady. I attended a healing Mass, which was exactly what I needed for my wounded feelings. Though I had been feeling alone through most of the Mass, by the end of the evening, Our Lady was with me. I was lifted up again when a member from my prayer group brought me over to her cousin to tell her of my experience. It seemed as if Our Lady placed one, then another, then another, within earshot of what I was saying. Before the night was over, the encouragement I received to spread Our Lady's message was stronger than ever, and God's army of intercessory prayer warriors were soon to be my new and closest friends.

When I was leaving Medjugorje in March of '84, Fr. Svet asked me to call a woman from my area whom he never met, but traveled alongside of her daughter, two years prior. When I called this woman, Joan, there was an immediate bond that connected us and a trusted friendship and love for one another that could only come from God. Joan and I were invited to several prayer groups to witness, as word spread about how her daughter was healed through Our Lady's intercession, and I am honored to share Joan's witness:

"The thing I remember about that first day was that it was a beautiful, crisp, sun-filled day. I was sure nothing could go wrong but, to my horror, the biopsy performed on a node from the neck of my daughter, Kim, showed Hodgkin's disease, a form of cancer. Time seemed to stand still, even though my mind and emotions were in high gear. How could this be happening to us? But this is not the beginning of my story.

"It was June of 1982, and our daughter was graduating from college. We wanted something special for her graduation gift. My husband and I decided upon a trip to Europe. Plans were made and, in August, Kim and a friend began their trip.

"On the plane, she sat next to a priest, though she was unaware that he was a priest at the time. His name was Father Svetozar Kraljevic, and he was going home to his native Croatia. They enjoyed a friendly conversation throughout the trip. When Kim returned home, she told me all about her meeting with 'Fr. Svet' and that he had given her a rosary to give to me. I was very touched by this gesture and wrote to thank him.

"Fr. Svet returned a letter to me telling me of a most extraordinary event occurring in Yugoslavia, in a small town called Medjugorje. He said the Blessed Virgin Mary was reportedly appearing daily to six children. He told of her requests for prayer, conversion, repentance, and fasting. I was intrigued and wanted to hear more. He also said that he felt it was God's will that we all had met and that one day I would come to Medjugorje to pray.

"Spring of 1983 arrived and with it the deepest valley of my life. My daughter was found to have Hodgkin's disease and I was stunned. Doctors were visited and plans were made during the first couple of weeks to fight this disease. I think I prayed every prayer I know and asked the Lord to cure my daughter. I was depressed. I could not sleep nights and walked the floor praying and beseeching God's mercy. One night, at about three o'clock in the morning, I prayed to the Lord and released Kim into His Hands. I asked that He make me strong for whatever it was I might have to face, and I went to bed. I was never depressed again! There were anxious moments and upsetting times, but no depression.

"Kim's disease was diagnosed as Hodgkin's disease, 3-B stage, stage 4-B is the most severe. Average treatment was about one year of chemotherapy, sometimes more. She began receiving two treatments each month. These made her very ill. She became exhausted and the treatments became difficult for her to endure. There were times when her white cell count would be too low to continue and a break in treatment would be necessary.

"Although no one had ever confirmed the apparition of Medjugorje to me, I felt moved to write to Fr. Svet, telling him what had happened in our lives and asking for his prayer that the Blessed Virgin Mary would intercede before Our Lord for Kim's healing. Our Holy Mother had always been a powerful intercessor in my life in the past. Even growing up and in my earlier adult life, I could relate to Mary. I felt she was the only one in Heaven who could possibly understand me.

"Time moved on. November came and Kim told me that her white cell count was too low again and that she was to receive mini treatments. These would not make her ill, and she would like to go for them accompanied by her friends. I never doubted her for one moment. After all, who would fool around with cancer?

"That same month I received a package from Fr. Svet. The package contained a blue polyester shirt that one of the nuns had purchased for him. He explained that he gave it to the visionaries to bring before the Blessed Virgin. The visionaries told him that Our Lady touched the shirt in blessing. He asked that I have Kim wear it. Kim flatly refused. She was angry that God had allowed this to happen to her. I put the shirt aside. There seemed to be an army of people praying for Kim, and the rosary was our weapon. The week before Christmas 1983, I found out that Kim had not been honest. She had not gone for treatment since the first week of November. She refused to go for any more treatment.

"After much pleading, she consented to speak with her doctor. I asked her once again, as a favor to me, to please put on the shirt. This time she did. She wore it to the hospital. Her doctor was most kind and understanding. He suggested a new chemotherapy which would not make her sick. An appointment was made for a treatment during the week between Christmas and the New Year. The night before her scheduled treatment, my daughter did not come home.

"When I caught up with her, she told me she would rather die than have any more chemotherapy. Since she was over 21 years of age, we had no legal right to force her. We would have had to go through a process to declare her incompetent. After talking with her doctor, who explained that we had to find out her present condition, Kim agreed to a CAT scan.

"An appointment was made and, unbelievable as it seems, it was cancelled again due to the machine not operating properly. A third appointment was made and kept. We were very concerned because now it was past the middle of January and Kim had not received chemotherapy for quite some time. It was a very dangerous situation. When it seemed as if we'd hit rock bottom, it was as if Our Lord reached down into that valley and lifted my daughter and our whole family out of the depths, for Kim's CAT scan showed her body to be totally free of cancer.

"As I am writing this witness, in 1987, it has been three and a half years since Kim was first diagnosed. My daughter is well, married and has a beautiful daughter whom she has named Mary.

"Just as Fr. Svet had written long before, I visited Medjugorje to pray, and also in thanksgiving to the Blessed Virgin Mary for her intercession for Kim. To my amazement, I was able to be in the room with the children at the time of the vision. What an unbelievable blessing and honor. God is so good!

"When I remember a 'chance' meeting on a plane, and a humble servant of God who gave a gift of his rosary and realized that that was the beginning of a miracle of God, it never fails to amaze me and to increase my faith."

As Joan and I witnessed together, I was blessed to hear of another confirmation of a healing, through Kim's shirt that was blessed by Our Lady in Medjugorje from my friend, Loretta Broughal. This is Loretta's testimony:

"My son, Peter, was born on June 25, 1985. When he was about five months old, I noticed a growth under his tongue. I took him to the pediatrician and was promptly sent to a pediatric mouth surgeon. The doctor said he would need surgery if it continued to grow. His tongue would be raised to the roof of his mouth without surgery. The doctor also said if the growth happened to break, he was to go to the emergency room immediately, as it contained poison.

"At this time a friend of mine, Kay, asked me to attend our parish's Sodality of Our Lady meeting. That night the guest speaker was a woman named Joan (a friend of Penny Abbruzzese, from our parish.) Joan began to tell us a story about her daughter. Kim had met a priest while traveling to Europe after her college graduation during the summer of 1982. Kim did not know, when they started talking, that he was a priest. He was going back to his homeland from his assignment of Sts. Cyril and Methodius Church in New York City. The priest was Father Svetozar Kralejvic (Fr. Svet). During that conversation, he gave Kim a rosary to give to her mother.

"Joan spoke of how she wrote to Father Svet and thanked him for the rosary and continued her witness which was recounted in the above story entirely by Joan. As Joan was telling her story, you could hear a pin drop in the cafeteria which was filled to capacity. Joan was very gracious and humble and passed the blessed shirt around the cafeteria for all of us to see and touch. When the shirt came to me, my friend Kay said, "Touch it, and when you go home, put your finger in Peter's mouth." When I arrived home, I picked up the baby, put my finger in his mouth, and said a Hail Mary.

"Several days later, I came home from work and noticed the growth was gone in the baby's mouth. I asked my mom, who was watching Peter, if it had broken and she said, "No." I was totally confused and couldn't understand how it just disappeared. That evening I called Kay to share the wonderful news with her. Kay said to me, "Did you put your finger in his mouth as I suggested during the Sodality meeting?" At that, I realized what had truly happened!

"My mother had a great devotion and love for Mary. She taught my brothers and me so much about the Blessed Mother and to always turn to her in a time of need. I knew in my heart of hearts that it was a miracle for my son. There was no doubt! The next day I called the doctor. He said that, medically, he had no explanation why the growth was gone.

"I read that the Blessed Mother in Medjugorje said she wanted her feast day to be celebrated on June 25, and she was to be called the Queen of Peace. June 25 is my son's birthday!"

Chapter Six

Messages Taking Hold of My Heart

"Do whatever he tells you." (Jn 2:5) These are the words that resonated in my internal world when Father Svet summarized Our Lady's main message, "Do whatever he tells you." I knew in my heart that the messages of conversion, prayer, and penance were Christ's saying, "Come back to me." Our Lady, through her messages, was bestowing upon me the wondrous secret of the way to find Jesus. From the very beginning, when I first heard Our Lady's message that we were to pray and fast, there wasn't a doubt in my mind that I was to incorporate this message into my life if I wanted to come closer to God.

Being blessed with the tremendous gift of corresponding with Fr. Svet since my first trip in March of 1984 was a grace beyond belief. Here in the United States everything was very hush hush about Medjugorje. Other than Father's letters and the messages he was able to relate to me, I had no other source of hearing what Our Lady was saying to the world through these young visionaries. I asked many religious in our community, and they had never even heard of Medjugorje.

When Father wrote to me and said, "We have to follow Jesus as closely as possible. There is no one else to follow and no one can stand between us," Our Lady was teaching me how to follow Jesus and no one stood between us because the messages seemed to arrive as though on eagle's wings. I hungered and thirsted for every word Our Lady was saying. Upon hearing these messages, I would try to put them into practice. Father wrote and told me the message of Thursday, July 5, 1984: **"Dear Children! Today I wish to tell you, always pray before your work and end your work with prayer. If you do that, God will bless you and your work. These days you have been praying too little and working too much. Pray, therefore. In prayer you will find rest. Thank you for having responded to my call."**

Needless to say, I took every word of Our Lady's message literally. When I went to work in the mornings, I asked God to bless me and the work I was about to undertake. I was glad when I had to park my car two blocks from my office. Here I was, with my little blue prayer book, and now I could walk to work reading my morning prayers. It was a beautiful feeling.

I asked God to share in my day. I never thought to do that before. The words that I read suddenly began to take root in my heart. I no longer needed to read my prayers. My walk to work became a dialogue with God through Our Lady. It was a priceless gem. As I sat down at my desk, I'd write a little note to Our Lady and share what was on my mind and pray she would be with me throughout the day. I would sign it, *Your daughter, Penny,* and then in steno code I'd add *I love you.* My days began to take on new meaning. I no longer felt burdened or alone with any difficulties that came my way. In my prayers, I asked God to inspire me with a spirit of joy and gladness and that's exactly what filled my heart. Our Lady's message simply taught me how to take time to pray, and how to take time for God.

Our Lady's message of July 12, 1984, blessed me with a new awareness. Our Lady told the visionaries, **"Dear Children! These days Satan wants to frustrate my plans. Pray that his plan not be realized. I will pray my Son Jesus to give you the grace to experience the victory of Jesus in the temptations of Satan. Thank you for having responded to my call."** It was during this time that I spent the entire summer reading from the collected works of St. Teresa of Avila. As a child, I was taught about the devil. Subconsciously, however, I had erased him from my mind. Throughout the years, this became easy because preaching about the evil one from the pulpit was nearly abandoned.

The teachings of St. Teresa brought me back into focus with the reality of the devil. The saint warned that, "The devil directs his attacks so that the soul gives up prayer." He tried this throughout the summer by creating considerable distractions. I underlined St. Teresa's thoughts about the devil.

"The devil puts so many dangers and difficulties into the beginner's head that no little courage, but a great deal, is necessary in order not to turn back, and a great deal of assistance from God." During that summer, I was very tempted to continue doing something in the wrong that was very easy to get away with. I knew it was unfit and, looking back, I can now see the devil was whispering, "Go ahead, you're too deep into it. God will never forgive you now." Well, when Our Lady's message was that she will pray to Her Son that He will give me the grace to experience His victory in Satan's temptations, I believed it with all my heart. Through the grace of Our Blessed Lord's Divine forgiveness in the Sacrament of Reconciliation, I was ready to ask for the courage that St. Teresa spoke about in order to discontinue what I was caught up in. Through Our Lady's intercession, the warning from St. Teresa to be aware of the temptations of the devil, and the assistance of God, the victory of Jesus was realized.

St. Teresa wrote, "I pay no more attention to devils than to flies. I don't understand these fears, 'The devil, the devil,' when we can say, 'God, God' and make the devil tremble." I thank God for the gift of St. Teresa's teachings because when I read the message of July 19, 1984, Our Lady reinforced that peace. **"Dear Children! These days you have been experiencing how Satan is working. I am always with you, and don't you be afraid of temptations because God is always watching over us. Also, I have given myself to you and I sympathize with you even in the smallest temptation. Thank you for having responded to my call."** I was so moved by that. I imagined that a mother could have no greater love for her child.

Father Svet wrote, "Once, as Blessed Mother was praying for the unbelievers with the visionaries, a large tear came out of her eye. As she was leaving, she said: **"Pray my children, it is not going to be easy for me."** And she left crying. When I read this, I immediately became sad. I felt so close to Our Lady, and my reaction was the same as when I saw my own mother crying. There wasn't anything I wouldn't have done to save her from that pain. The tears that accompanied my mother's broken heart when she lost her son instinctively brought to mind Our Lady's heart crowned with thorns and the tears that she must shed for all of her children who are lost. In my prayers, I implored, "What can I do, O Blessed Mother? What can I do to help ease the pain?" I knew the answer in my heart was what I had heard from the very beginning: pray and fast and offer up all of your sacrifices to God. I began to set aside an hour a day for prayer, and I thought about giving up pizza, which I love, as a small sacrifice for Our Lady.

The request in the message that I received from Medjugorje via Fr. Svet on August 14, 1984, was one that I did everything to try to avoid. **"I would like the people to pray along with me these days. And to pray as much as possible! And to fast strictly on Wednesdays and Fridays, and every day to pray at least one rosary; the joyful, sorrowful and glorious mysteries."** Our Lady asked that we accept this message with a firm will. She especially requested this of the parishioners and the faithful of the surrounding places.

Now I was looking to get out of that one. I imagined I could never pray all three rosaries. I could fast on bread and water on Wednesdays and Friday, a continued grace for me by now. Praying for an hour a day was a joy because it usually was towards the end of my night. I looked forward to that as my time to open my heart to God. Every day since 1983 when I had been given my rosary, I would say one rosary. But three? No way! I'd never find the time.

As usual, when I received a letter from Fr. Svet, I would call my angel here on earth, Sister Mildred, and share with her what Father had to say. Sister's conviction of the reality of Our Lady's apparitions, and the excitement of hearing the latest messages, was an inspiration to me and I always cherished Sister's wisdom. When I read to Sister that Our Lady asked us to pray three rosaries a day, she immediately said, "You know, Penny, she is asking that of you." Sister's remark was all I needed to hear. I had been looking for the easy way out. Here I was telling the Blessed Mother I would do anything for her, and when she asked for three rosaries, I tried to pretend that message must be for the villagers in Medjugorje, not for me. Sister's saying, "Penny, she is asking that of you," gave me the grace to accept this message with a firm will. Deep within I said, "Yes, but please Mother Mary, you have to help me find the time."

I had not yet discovered Our Lady's strength. As I asked her to help me find the time to pray more, it was no sooner said than done. In the past, I loved to watch television. Often my evenings were planned around my favorite sitcoms. Now, without realizing it, I had no desire to watch television at all. As I watched, I'd be thinking, "I could be praying." I realized what a precious gift spare time was, and that I should use this gift for God. Simple as that. I had always a great ability for making life complicated. Through Our Lady, the grace to turn off the set was gently bestowed and Christ's words became alive to me: *"And whatever you ask in my name, I will do, so that the Father may be glorified in the Son. If you ask anything of me in my name, I will do it."* (Jn 14:13-14) I asked for the time to pray, and it was granted.

I began to reflect how Our Lady, in just one short year, had so very gently advanced me in prayer. It started with one decade of the rosary. Then, as I wanted to know more about Our Lord, I was introduced to the mysteries of the rosary. As I was doing my readings and groundwork to be baptized in the Spirit in my prayer group, which is simply praying for an outpouring for *"The fruit of the Spirit which is love, joy, peace, patience, kindness, goodness, faithfulness, gentleness, self-control,"* (Gal 5:22.) an unintelligible desire for these gifts grew within me. God offers this baptism in the Holy Spirit to people who need only to reach out and receive in order to be on fire to fully serve Him. I wanted to fully serve Him!

During our weekly seminar, preparing for our baptism, we were asked to read a little bit from The Bible each day. A love for the scriptures blossomed through that commitment. When John, David, and I were in Medjugorje, Our Lady increased my prayers when we were told to daily pray at least seven Our Fathers, seven Hail Marys, and seven Glorias, and the Apostle's Creed. The following months, I began to value the hour of prayer at night that helped me give back to God all the little trials and tribulations I experienced during the day. It was this interior prayer for at least a half hour every morning and evening that strengthened my conscience. Our Lady once said to one of the visionaries: **"Your days will be different according to whether you pray in the evening or not."** My days were different as I followed Our Lady's instructions through the gospel of Mt: 6:24 & Mt: 6:34; *"No one can serve two masters. He will either hate one and love the other, or be devoted to one and despise the other. You cannot serve God and mammon"* and "Do not worry about tomorrow; tomorrow will take care of itself."

While preparing dinner and cleaning house, I would sing with tapes of praise and thanksgiving that David's mother gave me. I was delighted when I was told, "When you sing, you pray twice." Something wonderful was happening within me, and I didn't want to let it go.

Someone once said to me, "Don't you think all of those Hail Mary's are a bit too much?" My answer was, "There is no way I would ever give it up because I heard and I truly believe, 'Every time we say, Mary, she says, Jesus.'" The rosary was my treasure. Our Blessed Mother's words to the children on August 23, 1984, were simply, **"Pray, Pray, Pray."** St. Teresa of Avila said, "The Lord always provides the opportunity if we desire to pray. Prayer is an exercise of love." Through prayer, guided by Our Lady, my love for Jesus slowly blossomed like a bud.

I wanted to learn more about Jesus and His great love for us, so I prayed for a teacher or a "Spiritual Director." St. Teresa spoke of the necessity of a Spiritual Director if we wanted to advance in prayer. She relates, "For the Lord will provide one on the condition that all is founded upon humility and the desire to do the right thing." I'm still learning what humility is, but my desire to do the right thing is what joined my hand to Our Lady's. And so, I was blessed with a Spiritual Director before the summer was over and wouldn't you know, the first lesson I was taught was the "Humility of Jesus!"

Chapter Seven

Prayer and Obedience

"What can ultimately trouble the soul that accepts every moment of every day as a gift from the hands of God and strives always to do his will?" These pearls of wisdom were quoted countless times by a saintly priest with whom Our Lord and Our Lady so graciously blessed me as my spiritual director. Fr. Walter Ciszek's direction in my life was undoubtedly a miracle with which I was graced, truly a gift from the hands of God.

Fr. Ciszek, S.J., was an American-born Jesuit priest who survived for twenty-three years, unknown to family or friends, in the controlled society that existed in the Soviet Union. In 1939, he sought admission to Soviet Russia incognito, desiring to serve the people as a priest. In 1940, on March 19, he entered Russia but was arrested by the Secret Police a year later. Fr. Ciszek was required to endure fifteen years of inquisition and imprisonment as a "spy of the Vatican." After spending five years in solitary confinement in Lubianko Prison, Moscow, he was sent to the Siberian slave-labor camps above the Arctic Circle. Fr. Ciszek was declared legally dead in 1947 here in the United States. In

1955, upon his release from prison, he was permitted to live in the Soviet Union as a socially undesirable nonperson, to make a meager living as a common laborer. He functioned as a priest while working in factories and as an auto mechanic.

With incredible faith and trust in God throughout those years, Fr. Ciszek not only retained his sanity, but he was also able to turn the adverse forces of circumstances into a source of positive value and use those circumstances as a means of drawing closer to Our Divine Lord. Father's courage could have come only from the Holy Spirit as he said Mass under cover, in constant danger of discovery. He heard the confessions of hundreds who could have betrayed him. But his incredible hardships never surmounted his indomitable faith.

When I asked Our Lady just a year prior, "How do I pray?" little did I know I was to be taught by an extraordinary, humble servant of God who, without a spiritual book in all of those twenty-three years, considered his experience in the Russian camps as a "school of prayer."

I first met Fr. Ciszek in June of 1984 when my friend, Agnes, invited me to a gathering in which Father, whom she had known for a long time, was also present. I was deeply touched by his extraordinary warmth and simplicity. He was a wonderfully joyous little man, with sparkling blue eyes. His sense of humor and boyish laughter filled me with admiration and love.

In September, I was invited to visit with Father where he lived near Fordham University in the Bronx. I couldn't believe that I was watching the New York Mets play baseball with a priest, and not just any priest but one who had spent twenty-three years under the Communist regime.

Fr. Ciszek was the spiritual director of my friend, Tom, with whom I went to visit Father. On our drive to the Bronx, Tom mentioned his concern for my fasting. I thought it was funny since it was no problem for my husband, Mike. Yet, Tom was a friend, and I didn't want to ignore his concern for my health. I was not only fasting on Wednesdays and Fridays, but a few months prior, I had asked for the grace to fast on Mondays, too, for a very special intention. Tom reiterated what he had said many times before, "If you're going to continue fasting, you should have a spiritual director."

During the time I was under the spiritual direction of Fr. Ciszek, the joy of being in his company brought forth an overwhelming experience of confidence and trust as I shared with him about matters both big and small. On this my first visit with Father, he interjected comments here and there that made it seem as if he knew who I was and why I was there. I wasn't even sure why I was there. I wondered if Our Lord and Our Lady had arranged that afternoon. Father confirmed my thoughts by sharing with me that, "All things on this earth are governed by God's providence, and not man's effort."

Tom encouraged me to ask Father if he would pray about directing me. When I said, "Father, you would really have your work cut out for you." He responded, "I know what I'll do. I'll use a big ball of cotton or a feather duster!" The gentleness in his answer wiped away all my anxieties. As Father spoke about the love of God and his great love of prayer, his face was luminous. He was nearing eighty, but in his own words he was "...like a little kid when I speak of Our Lord." I smiled as I recalled from scripture (Mk 10:15): *"Amen, I say to you, whoever does not accept the kingdom of God like a child will not enter it."* Oh, how I admired his fervor.

I asked Father for his direction in regard to my fasting, and he listened very attentively to my reasons. For so many years, under the daily regimen of working to exhaustion in the camps, under the constant torture of hunger and cold, what came to him in the prison camps was a tremendous respect and love for the body. He said, "If the body is sick or sore, tired or hungry, or otherwise distressed, it affects the spirit, affects our judgement, changes our personalities. Even something as slight as a headache can affect our relations with those around us." Father's concern about my fasting was whether it affected my being totally present to Mike and the children. He was concerned for the lack of vitamins on the days that I fasted which could take its toll on me years later without my realizing it. He felt his arthritis could have resulted from the many years in the camps where the food ration was just barely enough to sustain life. He admitted the analogy was extreme, but he said that on the days that I fast, I should eat fruits and vegetables, in moderation. I have to admit that, interiorly, I truly struggled with his suggestion. I didn't try to refute what he said, but, in my heart, I was so sad as I thought, "But, Mother Mary, you said to fast on bread and water!"

The writings of St. Teresa of Avila and her explicit teachings on obedience echoed in my soul. "I often marvel thinking about learned men, religious especially, who after the labor it cost them to acquire their knowledge, use it to help me for nothing more than asking them, and that these are persons who don't want to benefit from this labor!" Fr. Ciszek had labored, and he was there to help me. My first lesson was obedience to Father's guidance. I received a priceless gift almost immediately - an appreciation of the little things in life that I always took for granted. Suddenly, eating an apple at dinner with my friends on a Friday, instead of breadsticks, was an absolute treasure. I had very rarely given thanks to God for the ordinary, but thanks to Fr. Ciszek, I was learning to thank God for everything: apples, bananas, peaches. A slice of lemon in a cup of hot water was suddenly a gift from God. As Father said about himself, "God is a very patient teacher, and I was a most stubborn pupil."

Sharing with Father that afternoon, my heart quickly grew softer and warmer. Words spilled from my heart like a free-flowing stream, expressing my desire to love God more.

I shared with Father how Our Lady was so very special in my life. We shared that common bond.

Fr. Ciszek was an internationally known director of "The Spiritual Exercises of St. Ignatius." The Spiritual Exercises are a compilation of meditations, prayers, and contemplative practices developed by St. Ignatius Loyola to help people deepen their relationship with God. He suggested that he would be able to teach me through the Spiritual Exercise. Through the exercises, he could teach me to be stabilized in God's love, "with a little leeway like the Empire State Building, because no one can be too rigid." I laughed as I thought, "Father, you must really love a challenge."

Father and I planned a date for beginning the exercise. I asked him if it would be all right if Agnes joined us. His delight that I included Agnes was obvious, and he hoped she would say, "Yes." Agnes knew in her heart that it was an invitation from God to spend this time with Father, and she agreed. Through the grace of the Holy Spirit and Our Lady of the Highways, my crippling fear of driving on parkways and over bridges, which was the only way to get to Fr. Ciszek, disappeared like a feather in the wind.

Our first week of instructions was absolutely beautiful. We had no idea what God had in store for us. We huddled over Father's shoulder as he read from the book of Genesis and explained to us the story of creation. It was fascinating. It was as if he was right there, and God was showing him how all was created. Father spoke of the order in the world before the fall of the angels. When he reached the part where God created the beasts, he described to us how the elephants rolled on their backs and scratched one another. The tranquility of the wildest animals seemed beyond our comprehension. His interpretations were so graphic that I prayed his teaching would never end. His joy of sharing and his love for scriptures permeated his every word and we were enraptured.

But week two was a disaster! Father had given us the book *The Spiritual Exercises of St. Ignatius,* and he gave us an assignment before we met again in ten days. I'm pretty sure that Agnes and I were on the same level in reading and writing and doing our assignment. My approach was haphazard, and that prevented me from taking the exercise as seriously as I should have. If I didn't understand something, instead of calling and asking Father's clarification, I simply omitted it. For example, the lessons were numbered, and I skipped numbers 48 through 64 thinking Father would explain them to me when we got around to it. It didn't work out that way. I thought as least I'd have Agnes to fall back on, but when Father said, "Okay, who wants to go first?" my heart stopped. I didn't know he was going to take us one at a time. I was first while Agnes went up to the chapel and prayed. That ninety minutes seemed like an eternity. Everything I had done the prior week seemed wrong. Father was very gentle, but very firm in letting me know I wasn't following the order of the retreat. By the time I came to the questions I had skipped, I wouldn't have blamed him if he'd booted me out the door. He corrected me with kindness, but I was so embarrassed. I just wanted to turn the clock back and be the old Penny when life was simpler. What did I know about colloquies and preludes? I thought, "Oh Mother Mary, are you sure you want me here? Maybe you have me mixed up with someone else. Perhaps someone sharper than I? Father didn't give up on me. He said, "Your present is your past, and your future is what you are now. So as of now, we'll try again."

It wasn't so much that I was embarrassed by my failure to understand the exercise. I resented the humiliation, and the bottom line was that my pride was hurt. I now understand the lesson that took me two and a half years to learn. Fr. Ciszek's book *He Leadeth Me* speaks of humility as truth. He writes, "It is only natural to resent humiliation. We recoil from humiliating experiences because they are an affront to the dignity of our person, which is another way of saying that our pride is hurt. That is the key to the problem, and it is then that we do well to recall who we really are and who God is. If we see nothing beyond the experience except the hurt and the unpleasantness, it can only be because we have lost sight, for the moment at least, of God's will and of his providence. So, we must learn to discern even in the humiliations, occasions for a deeper conformity to the will of God." I experienced a true lesson in humility, but at that time, I simply wanted to abandon ship.

When Agnes and I left Father's residence that afternoon, I knew by looking at her face that we were both on that same ship. We laughed so hard walking down the street, like two school children who didn't know how to handle a tiny measure of discipline. Agnes kiddingly said, "I'm not going back, I'm too embarrassed." We both said, "What are we doing this for, are we crazy? Who is St. Ignatius anyway?"

We went home wondering how to get out of going back. We thought of every excuse in the book, including death. We planned who was going to call Father and say, "Thank you anyway, but this can't possibly be for us." We had cold feet, yet, somehow, ten days later, we were back for round two. God is so good! Suddenly, the spiritual exercise began to take hold of our hearts as we looked forward to trying again.

Father taught us about the kingdom of God here on earth. I had never thought that as members of the Church, we were part of what he referred to as the Mystical Body, a community of believers. Father Ciszek referenced: "As members of that body, we cannot remain aloof or indifferent to others or to the good of the whole. Each of us must do our part to strengthen this body and extend this kingdom." I never thought that my role in the Church was significant until Father's teaching on the Mystical Body of Christ.

We learned the way of purification with God as the Creator and man as creature. We must acquire the infinite love of God and the absolute need of God for eternal life. He taught us about the fall of the angels and the sin of Adam and

Eve and its consequences, and the gravity and malice of sin against Our Lord. Through the grace of Our Lady, I began to understand. "Grace is simply God living through us," Father said. I began to put more effort into the responses. My colloquies, he told me, were very prayerful. I was shocked.

I learned so much about prayer from simple conversations with Father Ciszek. He said, "In prayer, we speak to God, and we ask his help. We seek his pardon, or we promise amends; we thank him for favors received. But we cannot pray as if we were talking to the empty air, so in the very act of praying we unconsciously remind ourselves of the reality and the presence of God, thereby strengthening our belief in him." He continued, "We cannot pray always in the sense of those contemplatives who have dedicated their whole lives to prayer and penance. Nor can we go around abstracted all day, thinking only of God and ignoring our duties to those around us, to family and friends and to those for whom we are responsible. But we can pray always by making each action and work and suffering of the day a prayer insofar as it has been offered and promised to God."

After Agnes and I had finished our exercise for the day, we would have lunch with Father. The joy and the blessing of sharing and listening brought us more knowledge of what faith was about simply through the breaking of bread.

Without our realizing it, God was zooming right in through St. Ignatius Loyola. To fulfill our assignments, we were to meditate, to learn this way of silence, of stillness, by a discipline that is most demanding. I doubted that I could ever be true to that, but I was limiting God.

Our work for the following week was a meditation on Hell. I was to see in imagination the length, breadth, and depth of Hell. I was to beg God for a deep sense of the pain which the lost suffer so that if, because of my faults, I forgot the love of the eternal Lord, at least the fear of these punishments would keep me from falling into sin. We were to reflect on five points and then share with Father the following week. The first point was to see in imagination the vast fires and the souls enclosed in bodies of fire. The second point was to hear the wailing, the howling cries and blasphemies against Christ Our Lord and against His saints. The third point was to use the sense of smell to perceive the smoke, the sulphur, the filth, and the corruption. The fourth was to taste the bitterness of tears, sadness, and remorse of conscience. The final and fifth point was to imagine the sense of touch, to feel the flames which envelop and burn the souls.

In all honesty, after four days of trying unsuccessfully to envision myself in Hell, I was about to give up. I would have done anything to avoid that assignment, but I knew that it was all part of my spiritual growth, and certainly Our Lady would not have given up. The thought came to go before the Blessed Sacrament and ask Our Blessed Mother for the grace to use all my five senses to taste, feel, hear, smell, and see the fires of Hell. *"Which one of you would hand his son a stone when he asks for a loaf of bread, or a snake when he asks for a fish? If you then, who are wicked, know how to give good gifts to your children, how much more will your heavenly Father give good things to those who ask him.*" (Mt 7:9-11) Our Father in Heaven blessed me with the fear of Hell, which to this day, I shudder to think about. I not only identified with the pain of Hell, but also realized how many times God could have taken me during my lifetime as I chose to ignore Him. But He didn't. He spared me from the fires of Hell.

Father Ciszek's blessing was to be able to unite his cross with Our Lord's and to realize that every moment of every day is a gift from God. He shared how he had been stuck in traffic for three hours on the previous Sunday. Upon returning home, unquestionably exhausted, he collapsed into his chair, "Thanks, Lord, I owe you one!"

Eventually, Father's arthritic condition caused him unceasing pain. It didn't dissuade him from climbing two flights of stairs to meet us at the chapel for a private Mass, his every step accompanied by a labored breath but with a loving smile. Father likely knew God was going to call him home soon. Our good-bye that day in November of 1984 was prolonged, and there were extra hugs for us as he called us his children - an extra special blessing I felt from Our Blessed Lord.

On December 8, 1984, I visited Agnes after Mass. We were talking about Father's great love for the Immaculate Conception when the phone rang. Agnes came back into the room to say that Father died during the early morning hours.

He was found in his green chair, head slightly tilted to one side, with no trace of distress on his face. It seemed as if he truly fell asleep in love. Father Ciszek's life of faith and love, rooted in the Hearts of Jesus and Mary, was the source of his constant joy and unfailing kindness to everyone he met.

Father taught me to stop, look, and listen, and I stop to say thank you to Our Lord and Our Lady for Father Ciszek in my life. I look up to the Heavens and know, dear Mother of God, that Father is among the Angels and Saints. He was with them even before his cause for canonization was initiated. And through the grace of the Holy Spirit, I gaze upon Father's picture and listen to the sound of his laughter which will always be a gift in my life.

Chapter Eight

The Need to Return

"He giveth quietness." (Job 34:29) To be still, to be quiet, are qualities that I dream of but fail to achieve. My family calls me "Phone Lady." That name attests to the difficulty of my quest to be still. I go through a tug-of-war with Our Blessed Lord. He offers the quiet, and I strive for more activity.

Independence, not one of my strongest characteristics, is also an irony. God creates opportunities for me to do things on my own, and I put His invitation to be self-reliant aside by asking a small army to join me. But that, as I'm sure God knows, is me. Those in the Heavens probably laughed then when they realized Our Lord's plan for me to go alone to Medjugorje.

A year had passed since my trip with John and David in March of '84, and I was still like a child in love. I couldn't get Our Lady or that special little village out of my mind. On Ash Wednesday, the anniversary of our pilgrimage with David, I prayed to Our Lady to bring me back to her again if it was God's will. A few of my friends expressed an interest in joining me but, for one reason or another, no one could make it.

Mike thought I was joking when I asked him if he would mind if I went alone. His concern was that I would be traveling in a Communist country by myself. Where would I stay? I didn't know. I couldn't drive a stick shift car, so that left out the possibility of my driving a rented car. A bus connection was available from the airport to Citluk, the town before Medjugorje. It had taken John and me three hours to drive from Dubrovnik to Medjugorje by car. I imagined it would take forever by bus. I dreaded the thought of asking for time schedules and directions at a bus terminal in Yugoslavia with sixty pounds of luggage and a Croatian dictionary in my hands. Yet, I couldn't think of any other way. I felt that God knew my desire to go. If I were meant to get there, it would all work out. Our Lord would open all the doors. My job was simply to trust Him. That, in itself, was a huge task for me.

My biggest concern was that my parents and my brother, Bobby, should be at peace about my trip. My mother, who hardly worries at all, was suddenly very concerned for my safety. My dad's fears of my traveling alone became larger than life. When Bobby tried to talk me out of going, I found that hard to understand. Then, I began to read between the lines. "What if you are put in jail? Mike and I would have to go there to bail you out." Though the effort to intimidate me failed, it blessed me with a tremendous insight as to how much he really cared.

I tried to put my family's worries aside and to reason with their fears. My mom and dad had lost their son just two years earlier; they were afraid I wouldn't come back. Bobby had been the one to identify Chucky. Air disasters that headlined the newspapers added to his anxiety. My dad voiced, "If you weren't traveling by yourself, I wouldn't worry." Dear God, I thought, is this a test? I prayed to Our Lady for help. I didn't want to hurt my parents or Bobby.

Two days before I was to leave for Medjugorje, on February 11, the feast day of Our Lady of Lourdes, my prayers were answered. I received a phone call from Yugoslavia, a first in itself for me, and the news that followed was my little miracle. The call was from Fr. Svet whom I had met in Medjugorje the year before. He had just read my letter saying I was coming back. When he told me to look for him at the airport, I thought I was dreaming. Father lived a good five hours from Dubrovnick, and I couldn't believe he would drive all that way to pick me up. During our short conversation, he mentioned a family who lived in the village that I could stay with. There was no need for my family to worry. My parents finally felt that I wouldn't be alone, and that made all the difference in the world to them. Our Lady knew my needs and the concerns of my family, as a loving mother would do, she answered each and every one of them.

Saying good-bye once again to Mike and our children at the airport filled me with a sadness that I tried hard to conceal. I still wasn't sure why I was going. It was simply a deep desire to return. Throughout the year, not a day had passed that Medjugorje didn't enter my mind. My thoughts were filled with the way the pilgrims responded to Our Lady's messages, **"Pray as much as you can, pray more and more. You can pray even four hours a day. Even if you do not understand. It is only one-sixth of the day. When I tell you to pray, pray, pray, you must not understand to mean just an increase in the number of prayers. I want to bring you to a deep desire for God."**

The miracle that I witnessed back in March 1984, was not the sun spinning, where looking directly at it seemed as if a host was in its center, with unbelievable colors emanating from it, or the illumination of the Cement Cross on top of Mt. Krizevac, that has no electricity on the mountain which is 1,800 feet above sea level. For me, the miracle I preserved, was the conviction of the pilgrims as they demonstrated their deep desire for God. Their faith clearly was deeply rooted. I saw countless men, women and children praying many evenings, spending one-sixth of their day in church.

In the past year, I'd remember the throngs of pilgrims who'd walked miles to a bus depot taking them back to their own villages, often at night with sub-freezing temperatures. It was not meeting the visionaries that had touched my heart and brought me back again. It was the faith of the people who, through Our Lady's intercession, were discovering just how much God loved them. I had witnessed Our Lady's first message, faith.

The entire village of Medjugorje was sometimes referred to as a "Dramatized Living Gospel." *"Give and gifts will be given to you."* (Lk 6:38.) On arriving in Medjugorje, I was brought to my host family who, for the next ten days, gave a total stranger an unparalleled love that brought the Gospel to life. A scholar of the law tested Jesus by asking, *"Teacher, which commandment in the law is the greatest? He said to him," You shall love the Lord, your God, with all your heart, with all your mind. This is the greatest and the first commandment. The second is like it: You shall love your neighbor as yourself. The whole law and the prophets depend on these two commandments."* (Mt. 22:35-40) These two commandments were undoubtedly priorities in the lives of the family that made me feel like one of their own. They simply glowed when they spoke of "Boga" (God) and the "Gospa" (Blessed Mother). The beauty inside their hearts surfaced with their love.

It was hard to communicate at first, but we didn't give up. I cherish the memories of looking at pictures with their four children or playing cards on the floor in front of a coal stove and trying to figure out what I was playing. We shared laughter while putting a tin can on the head of a snowman we made, making it easy to forget any language barrier.

When I came home from church in the evenings, I felt an almost indescribable warmth at being part of this family. I'd meet other English-speaking pilgrims and invite them back to the house to meet my family. Without even asking if they were hungry, the pilgrims would be invited to sit down to a full-course meal. My host family was not well-to-do, but whatever they had, they shared. All four children and the grandmother slept in one bedroom so that they would always have a spare room for a pilgrim. Their family life would never be their own again, but it didn't matter. This is what they felt the Gospa was calling them to do, and that was foremost to them.

Our Lady's instructions, which apparently the husband and wife used for guidance, were: **"If you want to be very happy, lead a simple, humble life, pray a great deal, do not delve into your problems, but leave God to resolve them."** I imagined that was why they were so much at peace and able to say no matter what happened, "No problem!" Their happiness was the fruit of their prayer life. I learned so much about family prayer from this special couple simply by their example. Not a meal was eaten, even if only bread and water, without first giving thanks to God, accompanied by their traditional grace of an Our Father, a Hail Mary and a Glory Be to the Father. Each evening after dinner, with the children nestled on our laps, we would all take part in a family rosary alternated in English and Croatian.

Our Lady has said on May 1, 1986, **"Dear children! I beseech you to start changing your life in the family. Let the family be a harmonious flower that I wish to give to Jesus. Dear children, let every family be active in prayer for I wish that the fruits in the family be seen one day. Only that way shall I give you all, like petals, as a gift to Jesus in fulfillment of God's plans. Thank you for having re-**

sponded to my call." I envisioned each member of this family as the unitive petals of a delicate rose who responded to Our Lady's message with a true commitment and great love. When Jozo, the husband, sat with the children for a few moments each day reading from their Bible, he didn't have to ask for their attention; it was undivided.

I witnessed Our Lady's message of prayer innumerable times throughout my stay. One morning, I was preparing to go back to New York, and we were having coffee before leaving at 3 a.m. for the airport. Jozo and his wife Marica finished their coffee and then said their morning prayers on their knees for about ten minutes. It was not done to impress me. It brought to mind how my dad had always begun his day with morning prayers on his knees. From that day on, I adopted their tradition.

As Our Lady said on November 15, 1984, **"Dear Children! You are a chosen people and God has given you great graces. You are not conscious of every message which I am giving you. Now I just want to say - pray, pray, pray! I don't know what else to tell you because I love you and I want you to comprehend my love and God's love through prayer. Thank you for having responded to my call."** The greatest grace among the many that the villagers of Medjugorje received was the prayer which nurtured their desire to return God's love and to do His will no matter what He asked of them.

On October 11, 1984, Our Lady's message was **"Dear Children! Thank you for dedicating all your hard work to God even now when He is testing you through the grapes you are picking. Be assured, dear children, that He loves you and, therefore, He tests you. You just always offer up all your burdens to God and do not be anxious. Thank you for having responded to my call."** The testing that Our Lady made reference to was a long rain in the middle of the harvesting season which caused great damage to the crops. I witnessed the villagers surrender their trials to God and learned a different significance of penance. I had no idea what kind of weather to expect when I went on my pilgrimage. I was totally unprepared for their coldest winter in one hundred and fifty years. As the temperature hovered near zero, the only source of heat was generated from a single coal stove in the living room. It was so cold that I was near tears as I went to bed. I thought of my family back home buried in mountains of blankets in their nice warm beds, and how I missed them. I struggled with the cold and thought of St. Teresa of Avila's words to Our Lord: "Is this the way you treat your friends? No wonder you have so few of them!"

I was told that Our Lady spent her afternoons praying at the top of Mt. Krizevac. On my first day back, it was snowing lightly, but I wanted to join Our Lady on the mountain to say thank you for bringing me back. Marica, the mother of my host family, pointed out the path from the road where she stood. I couldn't understand why she persisted in calling to me as I climbed, battling sharp thorn bushes. I kept turning around and waving, a little bewildered by her actions. Finally, her oldest daughter, Ivana, age 8, ran up the mountain to aid me. Marica had sent her so that she could lead me to a distinct and well-travelled path which marked the way to the Cross. God's path was so clear, and still I chose to go my own way and fall among thorns. I wondered, "Will I ever learn?"

After two years of trying to incorporate Our Lady's messages into my life, it took this trip to Medjugorje to truly show me how to live the messages. I believed that when I started praying the rosary and going to daily Mass my conversion was beginning and God would take over from there. Then I read a message that Our Lady gave on April 25, 1984, that made me realize that I have to pray to be converted each and every day. Our Lady said, **"Dear Children! Tell all my sons and daughters that my heart is burning for them. I ask only for conversion, only conversion. The word I tell the world is, be converted. I will pray to my Son not to punish the world, but you must be converted. You do not know, you will not know and cannot know, what God will send to the world; you must be converted. Renounce everything and be ready for everything. This is all I wish to tell the world: Be Converted!"** I knew I wasn't ready to renounce everything, and so I prayed to Our Lady to open my eyes so that I would be aware of my need for conversion. As I witnessed lines of pilgrims in the cold winter air waiting to have their confessions heard by Franciscan Friars in the open field, I saw Our Lady's message of conversion right before my eyes. I had a conversation with one man who had come to Medjugorje to initiate a scientific study of the apparitions. He shared that he had gone to confession for the first time in twenty-five years. The peace that he had received through this sacrament absolutely radiated from his being.

Fasting took on a new dimension as I shared bread and water with a community of believers who had sacrificed since 1981 as Our Lady had asked. I learned so much from their way of fasting and uniting their spirit of fasting with Christ. One of the villagers spoke about the many ways of fasting that had been traditionally handed down. Not eating meat for forty days, or not drinking their delicious home-made wine throughout Lent were minor offerings for the people in this village. They were happy to be called to the table of deprivation. Our Lady has said, **"The world has forgotten the value of fasting and prayers. With fasting and prayer, wars could be stopped and natural laws suspended. Only the seriously ill are free from fasting. Fasting cannot be replaced by prayer and almsgiving except by those who are very ill. You should pray and fast on behalf of the sick. It is easy for God to heal them but not easy for men."** (July 21, 1982.) Our Lady's message was prayer and fasting. Giving alms was the villagers' way of saying, "I have abandoned myself to you, Lord."

Our Lady's first message to the children in June of 1981 had been, **"I am the Queen of Peace, I have come to bring peace to the world"** The peace that Our Lady promised permeated this small remote village and filled the hearts of the villagers with the grace to love without fear. For Our Lady has said, **"Love is peace, peace is love."** I was still searching for that peace by which I was surrounded.

Our Lady had provided this extraordinary time alone, and I could no longer ignore it. It was for a purpose. Gradually, I began to feel truly at ease in the presence of Our Lord. I begin to realize the beauty of silence. I prayed to Mary to show me how to practice being silent. After all, she was my perfect example. When she was told by Simeon in the temple during the Presentation of the Child Jesus, *"and you yourself a sword will pierce so that the thoughts of many hearts may be revealed."* (Lk 2:35), she remained silent. Later, when she went forth with Jesus to Calvary and stood at the foot of His Cross listening to His final breath, she remained silent. What greater examples than that did I have?

One afternoon, while I was in the apparition chapel, I was asked if I could stay and be present during Exposition of the Blessed Sacrament. Those two hours seemed like twenty minutes. I could hardly describe the peace I felt from being quiet. In this very holy room, with the Blessed Sacrament a few feet away from me, joined with Our Lady's silence, I was filled with grace and experienced a profound peace. My face felt heated, as if sitting by a blaze, as the thought came to me, *"Pause a while and know that I am God."* (Ps 46:10)

One of the priests came into the chapel to put away the Blessed Sacrament, and I was the only one left in the room. The visionaries would enter soon, and I was thinking that there was something missing. The table was bare. Last year, there were so many articles placed on the table to be blessed by Our Lady. Since the articles that people had left in the room during the day remained near the far wall, I decided to set the table. I felt so honored doing this for Our Lady. While lighting the candles, I wondered if Our Lady might be in the room early.

My ten-day stay in Medjugorje passed as a breath in the wind. I knew that this time it would be very hard for me to leave what seemed like a place where Heaven and Earth meet. As I said goodbye to Sr. Janja, I was given a little Baby Jesus blessed by Our Lady to take home for David. A year had passed, and his condition was the same, although this time I knew that God was allowing David to be used in a very special way. Throughout the year, people came to work with David in a program to stimulate his muscles. I'd witnessed them praying while they were working his arms and legs, trying to get a message to his brain so that he would be able to crawl. Many of the volunteers said they'd come to know prayer only through working with David. For so many, that was their prayer time. I recalled Sr. Janja's words from last year, "Mary gives you hope," and I was able, during this trip to see a far brighter horizon of hope. Hope that David would walk someday, and hope that I, too, would learn to walk the gospel as Our Lady had shown me through the villagers in this special parish in Medjugorje.

I walked home from church my last evening there to find a group of men and women coming from Mass heading towards their homes. They prayed and then sang, and I wished the world could see how happy they were. Their deep desire for God carried their tunes like the birds in spring. I cried with joy because I knew in my heart that the Gospa was guiding their steps.

My favorite star was twinkling brighter than ever. From the first night that I walked home and became lost in the dark, the twinkle in that particular star had reminded me of the twinkle in Fr. Ciszek's eyes, and so I called my star, Fr. Ciszek. I never felt that I walked alone. The grace of God and the presence of Our Lady and the angels and saints seemed to embrace with love all who walked this Holy Ground.

Medjugorje was the classroom, and the Mother of God was my teacher. In Mary's hands, the Gospel of John came to life, and I was to behold it. For the first time, I truly heard His words: *"I give you a new commandment: love one another. As I have loved you, so you also should love one another."* (Jn 13:34) A gentle initiation into how to become a better Christian was made known to me as I was blessed with a deep love from perfect strangers during my stay. My steps throughout the village were accompanied by Christ.

From the hills of Medjugorje to a school of love, Our Lady gently guided me, through the visionaries, with her message: **"I am your Mother and I have come to earth to teach you to love."**

I was given a "new" commandment, even though I had heard it a hundred times before. Through the grace of God and with Mary to lead me, this "new" commandment gave new meaning to my life.

Chapter Nine

A School of Love

"Give and gifts will be given to you, a good measure packed together, shaken down, and overflowing, will be poured into your lap. For the measure with which you measure will in return be measured out to you." (Lk 6:38)

I thank Our Blessed Lord for the words that I heard when I first came back to my faith: "We can't go to heaven with our hands empty." Although I know that we don't have to earn heaven, it made a lot of sense that we would want to have something to offer Him when we face Him in Heaven. The gift of doing for others is really a contradiction in terms. On the surface, it seems that I am giving of myself, but the measure I receive through the love of others far exceeds my poor efforts.

We probably will never know in this world why certain people enter our lives at certain times, even if only for a moment. I used to think that they were "chance" meetings, but I've learned that providential is a more apt description. The dictionary defines providential as: "as if decreed by divine providence." Its synonym is lucky. I tell my children not to think in terms of being lucky but in terms of being blessed. They may not fully understand, but that's okay. It took me more than thirty years to realize how blessed I am. All the time, I thought I was just lucky.

One of my greatest blessings during my volunteer work at Mercy Hospital was meeting a patient in the Cancer Care Unit who, through Our Lady, inspired and helped me reach out a little further. Her name was Florence. That was a beautiful opening to start a conversation, for my baptismal name is also Florence. Florence mentioned that she had been working as a volunteer in United Cerebral Palsy Center (UCPC) in Nassau County for over thirty years. I asked Florence about her work with the handicapped. The love in her heart for the work she was doing was evident in every answer.

After my first meeting with Florence, I was anxious for the following Thursday to arrive. The evening progressed, and everything was quiet. I sat by her bed, and she shared heartfelt stories of a love that began when she was an aide feeding a young child thirty years before. She expressed the joy they each shared as she watched him develop in maturity through the years. Florence's stories of taking the young boy Christmas shopping year after year and spending special days picnicking with him in the park touched me in a profound way. I only had one more Thursday with Florence, for God called her home after that. But at least I was able to thank her for encouraging me to call for an interview to be a volunteer with the cerebral palsied. So, by providential design, Florence had planted the seed that God had given to her.

I visited the UCP Center in Roosevelt, Long Island, with a friend whose son attended the center. She showed me around the building. When we went into her son's classroom, assisting the teacher was a volunteer she knew. A sense of peace, joy and love filled the room. I didn't have to see any more than that. I knew in my heart that this center would be an answer to my prayer asking, "What can I bring up to God?"

Here, I thought, I could learn to give of myself other than volunteering in Hospice. But right away my selfishness surfaced. When asked what day I could volunteer, I responded that I would be available on Fridays. The volunteer in the classroom said, "Oh, if you could come on Thursday, we could really use you. We are short of help on that day."

To be perfectly honest, I was disappointed. The supervisor at my job had given permission for me to take a day off during the week to volunteer. I wanted it to be Friday so that I could have a three-day weekend! As I look back, I smile. I had prayed for Our Lady to be my guide, and here I was looking for a three-day weekend! Would I ever learn to just say yes as Our Lady did, without trying to find something in it for me?

So, I worked on Thursdays at United Cerebral Palsy Center during the day and at Mercy Hospital in the Cancer Care Unit during the evening. I came to cherish my

Thursdays. I felt so close to Our Lady on this day. Not only was it my special day, but Our Lady gives her message to the parish in Medjugorje on Thursdays. Now, after a full day at the UCPC and Mercy Hospital, homework still had to be checked, dinner still had to be prepared, and I still needed to be present for Mike and the children. But I felt alive, though sometimes totally drained.

When I first started to work at the Center, it was a replay of the nervousness that I experienced in the Cancer Care Unit. I wanted to do what I could, but God knew I was a chicken at heart. I honestly didn't know if I could handle the emotional end of it, but I was right there to run the errands that needed to get done.

A division of the UCPC is a workshop. This is where the adults who are qualified perform various jobs depending on their motor skills. For example, one section of men and women, eighty percent of them in wheelchairs, use a machine that puts metal rings around little plastic suction cups used for hanging ornaments. This job helps them feel useful. They receive a small stipend for the work, but more importantly, a bond is formed in this working relationship with one another. It is truly invaluable.

My first job at the Center was to help set up a quick line of breakfast rolls, danishes, and coffee for the "clients" - the name that is used when referring to those who attend the center. They'd come in from the workshop for their coffee break and quickly help themselves to the food. For me, it was great. I was separated from them by a six-foot table, the perfect space I needed to become acclimated to the surroundings. I thought I knew what to expect, but I quickly discovered that behind each smile and warm "Good Morning" was an extraordinarily special person.

So many of those on line were in wheelchairs, and I was astounded at how independent they were. Just to hand someone a cup of coffee was a learning and apprehensive experience for me. Many had twisted hands, and I had to position the cup of hot coffee perfectly. They knew the best way; I had to learn.

There were so many lessons to learn. I needed to take the time to listen to difficult speech, for if I filled in the words, they wouldn't persevere and would never be understood. I learned patience for I was not to hurry them or take their task and do it for them. Often, they needed time rather than help. I learned to stand beside them as they entered a new and untried venture, for their failures would be outweighed by the times they surprised themselves and me. I learned to ask them for their help, for their greatest need was to be needed. I realized that it was difficult for them to put their thoughts into words, and a mere smile or a word of encouragement was all that was needed for them to try once more. The greatest lesson I had to learn and practice with sincerity was to respect and love them just as they were, not as I wished they were.

Our Blessed Mother's message to the children in Medjugorje on May 29, 1986, was **"Dear Children! Today my call to you is that in your life you live love toward God and neighbor. Without love, dear children, you can do nothing."** I learned through Our Lady how to love in such a precious way, transmitted to me by the love of the disabled, those whom I had avoided in the stores or on the streets for most of my life. They needed to be like you and me. I became aware of the barriers I subconsciously constructed to hinder that end. Their determination, no matter how impossible a task might seem, taught me to respect and love these special brothers and sisters of mine.

A client named Viola broke the ice and gave me my first encounter with reality. I'd been asked to bring a walker every Thursday to her section of the workshop. Viola was in a wheelchair and her therapist, Pam, encouraged her to stand with the walker for five minutes with a short sit-down break, and then take a few steps in place. Viola was excited about standing up and, although it was a monumental task, she managed to do it. After the first week or so with Viola, I became more relaxed. She was filled with enthusiasm and loved to talk. I think those precious minutes were more a joy for me than for Viola. When Pam said how delighted Viola was to get out of the chair for those few minutes, her words spoke loud and clear to my heart. I realized that I take every step for granted, but to Viola it was a gift just to stand for a few minutes a week.

Eventually, Viola's ulcerated feet put an end to attempting to walk with a walker though she'd given it everything she had. She hid her disappointment like a needle in a carpet, barely visible. Though the physical therapy ended, a beautiful friendship for us began. Meeting Viola was the grace that allowed me to ask the Lord for an end to my complaining or at least to try to think twice before complaining. I will always recall Viola's excitement, her lighting up like a 100-watt bulb when she was about to get out of her chair. The pain that it entailed never suppressed her glow.

At UCPC, I was especially blessed to meet a little eight-year-old boy named Matthew. Matthew was my first feeding assignment. He could not communicate verbally. He was in a wheelchair and unable to feed himself. A spark of love ignited instantaneously when I first laid eyes on Matthew. His features reminded me so much of my four-year-old nephew, David, and their limited abilities were evenly matched.

I would talk while feeding Matthew, and his blank response somehow was easy for me to accept. Even though I never saw Matthew smile, I felt Matthew knew he was loved. Before I would begin to feed him, I would bless his forehead and silently say a special Hail Mary. I prayed that, out of each teaspoon of food that it seemed to take forever for him to swallow, he was getting the proper nutrients necessary to sustain him. After three months of feeding Matthew once a week, his teacher called my house the night before one particular Thursday. I wasn't home, so she left me a message simply saying she would see me tomorrow. When I came into the Center the next day, instead of waiting until eleven o'clock to go to Matthew's class, I stopped in at 9 a.m. His teacher gently told me that Matthew had died of heart failure. I went back to my job as an aide to the volunteer dentist, Dr. Shapiro, and told him that Matthew had died. He didn't know Matthew, but he knew the sorrow in my heart was great and that it was crushing me.

I wrote to Matthew's parents to convey my sympathy and received such an inspiring response. His family's grief was immense, but his mom wrote that she was expecting another child. She felt God's hand had closed a window in taking Matthew home but had opened a door with the coming of the new baby. Her reply was a great comfort to me. As I closed my eyes that night and prayed, I was filled with a tremendous amount of peace. I thought of Matthew in Heaven, playing with other children in a field of daisies, Jesus and Mary watching over them, and often playing with them.

The United Cerebral Palsy Center is set up like a school. The blend of the clients, teachers, aides, volunteers, and all who worked at the center filled the premises with a unique love that can only come from God. I was being educated at the UCPC as if I were in school. The more homework that I did there, which was simply to open my heart and know there are other lives in this world with special needs and a need to be recognized, the more knowledge I gained of God's love. It was my own School of Love.

A special time in my day at the United Cerebral Palsy Center was when I visited a classroom of twelve very special adults whom I am also graced to count as friends. Their understanding of one another's feelings creates a bond of devotion to each other that I can't imagine ever finding elsewhere. They revealed the Majesty of God through the love they showed towards one another. There were no prejudices, no barriers. They listened to each other. It's not easy for me to be still and listen. I've tried and I've failed, but God is so good and picks me up again, brushes me off, and interiorly, lets me know, through their understanding, that it's okay, we'll just try again.

Every time one of the clients, Tammy, sees the pin of Our Lady on my volunteer jacket she says, "Where would I be without Mother Mary?" She said that it is sometimes hard for her when people make fun of her because of her simplicity. She was easily frustrated. At first, the laughter bothered her to the point of tears. I would take Tammy to several Marian days of prayer. She stated to pray from her heart to Our Lady telling her that people don't understand her. It is only since praying, Tammy said, that it no longer bothers her. In 1 Peter, 4:14 it is written: "If you are insulted for the name of Christ, blessed are you, for the Spirit of glory and of God rests upon you."

My family was surprised at the spiritual awareness I was blessed with after Chucky died. The mystery of Our Blessed Lord's love for us blessed me with an inner peace. My family approached my new-found spirituality with extreme caution. For the longest time, they were afraid I might be going off the deep end. They couldn't understand where I was coming from or where I was heading. I became the object of jokes, and I wished that they might understand me. When I allowed my frustrations to turn into sorrow, I would recall Tammy's advice, "Tell Mother Mary." As I prayed from my heart to Our Lady, I felt confident that her touch had lightened my pain. Instead of wishing for my family's understanding, I needed Tammy's words to remind me what Our Lady has been saying as part of her message from Medjugorje, July 3, 1986, **"Dear Children! Today I am calling you all to prayer. Without prayer, dear children, you are not able to experience either God or me or the grace which I am giving you."** It took years, but, eventually, my family's laughter turned into questions and a new understanding began to take place. I thank Our Lady for that grace, for she is the Queen of the Most Holy Family. Some might say that Tammy's maturity is comparable only to that of a child. It was her childlike faith that is so precious to God.

I learned another lesson in the School of Love – a lesson learned as the result of a tremendous amount of pain caused by my own insensitivity. June of 1986 was the end of the school year for UCPC. I knew that I wouldn't see most of the familiar faces until school resumed in September, but it was different with my friend Mark.

Mark was in his mid-thirties, extremely articulate and a true joy. Because of his many physical disabilities, it was rare to see him even sit up in a wheelchair. Most of the time, due to problems with his spine, Mark lay on his stomach on a hospital gurney. Mark and many of our friends from the center lived in a nursing home located near my house. While leaving on the last day of school, I said to Mark, "I'll be in touch." I planned to see him over the summer at the nursing home.

Six weeks after school was closed, I made plans to visit my buddy Jimmy at the nursing home and take one of his friends to see him. An aide and I helped take them to dinner and, when we came back, I knew it was important for Jimmy and his friend to have time together to share, so, I decided I would go down the hall and visit with Mark.

At first, he seemed happy to see me. Then, his head went down, and he wouldn't look at me. I was holding his hand and his strokes unexpectedly gave way to strikes. I couldn't understand why he was hitting me, so I kept on saying, "Mark, what's wrong? You're angry at me for something, and I don't know what I did to upset you." I asked him to please tell me. Finally, I had to say, "If you can't tell me, I'll have to leave because I can't stay here with you hitting me."

The staff at the nurses' station saw that I was having a rough time, but Mark's strikes were not strong enough to cause me real physical pain. It was more the pain I felt in my heart at his striking me that caused me to want to leave. I pleaded with Mark one more time to please tell me what was wrong. Very slowly, he picked up his head ever so slightly. He was crying. He said, "You said that you would come to see me, and you never did." He told me he dreamed of me coming to visit so many times, and how much it hurt him because I never even called. The tears were streaming down my face. My heart was breaking because I had let him down.

I was explaining to Mark how there was no excuse, even though I was busy at home with Mike and our children during the summer. I should have at least called. He began to kiss and caress my hands with such tenderness. My tears flowed because Mark is human and is a man, and he is not afraid to love. I realized at that moment that God doesn't give us his greatest gift of love merely to restrict it to family. That special reserved love for our families should not inhibit our ability to love others; it should enhance it. St. Paul tells us in his letter to the Corinthians, 1 Cor: 13:2: "If I have the gift of prophecy and comprehend all mysteries and all knowledge; if I have all faith so as to move mountains, but do not have love, I am nothing." Through Mark, this lesson taught me not to be afraid to love. God is love, and God is eternal.

Taking Jimmy's friend back home, I passed by a chapel that has Perpetual Adoration which is the exposition of the Blessed Sacrament 24 hours a day. I went in and poured out my heart. My heart was filled with sorrow even though when we parted, Mark was happy. We had made plans for the following week for his birthday, but the pain that I had caused and that had made him cry stayed with me. Suddenly, I realized, it wasn't Mark who cried because of my selfishness, it was Jesus. Mark was Jesus. So many times, I would tell Jesus, "I'll be there, I'll be there," and then only turn to Him when it was convenient for me. How many times as I drove past the nursing home - too busy to stop in because of shopping or going to the beach - had I passed Jesus as He patiently waited for me to visit?

Before I left the chapel, I prayed for a sign that would indicate what Our Lady wanted to teach me. I felt in my heart that I was being taught a lesson from my experience with Mark. I thought of the cross on which Jesus died for my sins and had consciously tried to avoid the pain or the thought of Jesus suffering. The only time I would pray to Our Lord crucified was on Good Friday. Once a year was enough for me. In Medjugorje, as you climb the mountain called Mount Krizevac (Mountain of the Cross), it is marked with the fourteen Stations of the Cross. I had made the climb so many times, but I always avoided joining myself to Jesus' suffering because I didn't want that part of Christianity. I didn't want to feel His suffering. "Yet, it was our infirmities that he bore, our sufferings that he endured." (Is. 53:4)

As I left the chapel, my eyes fell on a book written by St. Alphonsus Liguori entitled *The Way of the Cross*. Here was a priceless gift that Our Lady wanted me to read. "The Way of the Cross" is a devotion to the Sacred Passion in which we accompany, in spirit, our Blessed Lord on His sorrowful journey from the house of Pilate to Calvary. We recall, with sorrow and love, all that took place from the time when He was condemned to death to His being laid in the tomb. "If anyone wishes to come after me, he must deny himself and take up his cross daily and follow me." (Lk 9:23)

From that day forward, I prayed for the grace to walk with Jesus and to follow "The Way of the Cross" by reflecting on the stations each day. I asked God for the strength to carry my cross daily, which is only a tiny splinter of wood compared to the cross on which Christ died for my sins.

Jesus' words to Our Lady referring to the Apostle John, "Woman, behold your Son" (John 19:26), bestowed Mary as our mother on all mankind. It is said that in Medjugorje, Our Lady spends her afternoons praying at the foot of the Cross. And she has asked us, through the visionary Marija, to "renew our prayer before the Cross." Her message continues, of February 1986, **"Dear Children! I am giving you special graces and Jesus is giving you special gifts from the cross. Take them and live! Reflect on Jesus' Passion and in your life be united with Jesus! Thank you for having responded to my call."** I learned how to love from those who, in their disability, have tremendous crosses to carry. They carry their crosses with love.

Chapter Ten

A Time for Healing

When I said that I would help spread Our Lady's message in the Church of St. James, I'm glad I couldn't see what it would entail. If Christ had shown me everything that I had to undergo, the sorting out of all my own feelings, I doubt if I would have said *yes*. As I tell about Our Lady's messages, I have failed to recognize my own struggle with the messages of peace and reconciliation.

I asked a particular priest in Medjugorje for his blessing. He felt I was carrying a splinter of Our Lord's Cross and that I received the strength to do so from His Mother. He added that my heart was in pain and that what was causing the pain was my need to forgive. He reminded me of how vital it was to believe that we must forgive those who trespass against us. As I reflected on this in prayer, I realized that different situations that arose relating to Chucky made it difficult for me to trust in God completely.

Chucky's sons, Brian and Stephen, visited us for a weekend during Easter vacation two years after Chucky died in 1983. I treasure the memory of every minute of the fun we had together. Sometimes, it was hard to believe that Chucky wasn't part of it. We prayed the rosary each night before they went to sleep. I treasured that, too.

I didn't plan to bring up Chucky's name while the children were around, yet so often the Holy Spirit seemed to include him in our conversations. One morning, as I was writing a short note to Our Lord and Our Lady to bless our day, Stephen, then seven, asked if he could write something. It was only through a grace from Our Lady that I was able to hold back my tears as I read his note - *Dear Mary and God, did you have a nice Easter up in heaven? And did my father have a nice Easter in heaven, too?* Moments like that made the pain of missing Chucky seem too much to bear.

I prayed to God that Brian and Stephen would never forget their Dad. They were so young when he died. I hoped his deep love for them would always be a picture in their hearts. The most difficult time for me was when it was time to take them home. So many of their ways reminded me of their father. I wanted to hold on to that as long as I could.

It wasn't until four years after Chucky died that I prayed to Our Lady. *Why is it every time my spiritual director mentions Chucky's name I fall apart? Why can't he leave well enough alone?* I was happy as long as the talk about Chucky didn't do more than scratch the surface of our relationship.

My director patiently helped me to understand that, no matter what I said, I would never really know why Chucky took his own life. I continued to shield his image after he died because it was important to me that no one think any less of him. My struggle to accept his death was deep and ongoing.

As much as I loved my brother, I unconsciously crossed the very fine line that separated love from hate. For three years after his death, I refused to admit to myself how angry I was that he did not say good-bye. My anger made me feel guilty. I knew he didn't deserve it, yet I couldn't let go.

We had always trusted each other and had always been there for each other. When we were teenagers, we'd rented a small boat and, after a beautiful day fishing, a sudden turbulent storm took us by surprise. I'll never forget Chucky's feverish efforts to reach the dock as the waves increased in ferocity. A fear of drowning was very real to me, but my trust in Chucky surpassed my fear.

Two years before he died, when he was only twenty-nine, his vivacious love for life took a one hundred and eighty degrees overnight turn. My mom called to say that Chucky was very sick. My first thought was that he was physically ill. That he could suffer mentally never entered my mind. While there must have been some prior indications, we obviously missed the signals. Our family had a habit of covering things up so as not to burden one another.

When mom and dad went to Chucky's house, they did not know what to expect. They found their son, who had always been their rock, a little frightened child, terrified by unreal imaginings that he and his family were in danger. His wife, Helen, said his paranoia had been evident for some time. She hadn't spoken of this to anyone because she could hardly believe it was happening.

Chucky finally agreed to see a doctor at a psychiatric center. He was at the point where he was paralyzed by his fears. Chucky suffered silently. In the two months that he was hospitalized, he would only communicate in one-word answers. The shock treatments, which were supposed to help him, added to his blank stare. He seemed to look right through you. He shuffled like an old man, which was the complete opposite of his usual quick pace.

As the time for his release approached, Chucky began sharing his anxiety with friends and relatives. What would tomorrow bring? He went home on weekend passes, but he said that leaving Helen and the boys to return to the hospital on Sunday nights took everything out of him. He wanted so much to feel better, and it hurt him beyond belief to be so incapacitated.

Two months after he came out of the hospital, my brother was filled with determination to overcome any anxieties. He seemed happier than ever to be back at work. Without a doubt, his surprise 30th birthday party in April 1981 was one of the greatest joys of his new life. But the paranoia that terrified him began to reappear a few months later as he faced the first anniversary of his breakdown.

His fears became colossal. We didn't know what to do next. My sister-in-law, Karen, suggested that we come with her to a healing Mass. Certain readings pertaining to healing and special prayer intentions would most times accompany a healing Mass. Often, the priests would pray over individuals for healing. Chucky agreed to go, even though it had been years since he had been to Mass. Neither he nor I had ever given any Mass the full attention that we gave to that Mass that evening.

A healing Mass was new to us, and we were a bit frightened by what was happening around us. As we stood before the altar, Chucky felt a feeling of electricity permeate him. We were a little unsettled and didn't know what to expect, but God eased our anxieties as the priest drew near. His warmth and tenderness poured forth a great surge of love as we immersed ourselves in prayer.

We were blessed with many healings that evening, and one was a year's extension of Chucky's life. The next year, in November 1982, the fear of his getting sick again around the same time of year, entered my heart. I asked him to be honest and tell me how he really felt. He responded, "Every now and then I get frightened that it will come back again, but I've got a handle on it." Throughout the years, I've wondered if Chucky's "handle" was his decision to make it easier for everyone else, even if the pain became unbearable for him, so that they would not worry about him.

When I was able to admit to myself how angry I was at Chucky for being so selfish in taking his own life, I realized that he couldn't be held responsible for his actions. His pain had to be excruciating. The mystery of mental illness and why God allowed such a thing to happen would never be mine to know. To know that I didn't suffer alone was a great gift that I received from Our Lady, Mother of Sorrows. I didn't know where else to turn and finally turned to prayer. The peace of Christ that I prayed for soon became a reality. I marvel at the way God leads us in all situations. Mary's message of October 2, 1986: **"Dear Children! Today again I am calling you to pray. You, dear children, are not able to understand how great the value of prayer is as long as you yourselves do not say: 'now is the time for prayer, now nothing else is important to me, now not one person is important to me but God.' Dear children, consecrate yourselves to prayer with a special love so that God will be able to render graces back to you. Thank you for having responded to my call."**

I saw my family being pulled apart by the tragedy of Chucky's suicide, and I felt helpless. Watching their pain was harder than bearing my own. My retreat to prayer in the evenings helped me to feel confident that God was in control and that He would take care of all of us, His children.

My worry had preempted my call to trust in the Lord, and I looked to Our Lady for help. I tried to imagine what it must have been like for her when the Angel Gabriel said, *"The Holy Spirit will come upon you, and the power of the Most High will overshadow you."* (Lk 1:35) The healing I needed was to submit to the will of our Heavenly Father. The grace to do so could be mine; all I had to do was ask for it.

So, I began to accept God's will and tried not to question Him any longer. One by one each of the heartaches I was experiencing became lighter. Although I was asked to bear only a sliver of Our Lord's Cross, I began to trust and truly believe that God wouldn't let our burdens grow too heavy for our strength.

To pray was my decision. Not to judge Chucky was also needed to be a decision. I thought of Our Lady in her perfect quietness as she listened to the crowd shout, "Crucify him, crucify him!" If the Mother of Our Savior didn't judge the crowd who wanted to put her Son to death, how could I possibly judge my brother? I needed to apply the scriptures to my own life when I read, *"Stop judging and you will not be judged. Stop condemning and you will not be condemned. Forgive and you will be forgiven."* (Lk 6:37)

I began to think about Our Lord's crucifixion, the heavy hammer smash that drove the nails through Christ's flesh, of the pain, of how difficult it must have been for Him to speak from the Cross when every word must have filled Him with a new wave of agony. Yet, He cried to the Father, *"Father, forgive them, they know not what they do."* (Lk 23:34)

Through prayer, I finally made peace with my brother. The moment I was able to say, "Chucky, I'm sorry for staying angry with you for so long," the love I had for him flowed back into my heart.

Up until this point, when I was asked to witness about Medjugorje and Our Lady in my life, my testimony touched only slightly on the tragedy I had experienced. I did not go into detail for a few reasons. First of all, the stigma of having a suicide in my family was a struggle for me. When preparing to talk to a large prayer group one evening, I commented to a friend that I felt it was important to mention Chucky's suicide; after all, it was a fact. He strongly suggested I leave it out, and so I did. After coming to terms with forgiveness, my director encouraged me by saying that I might be able to help others who have been peeking out from under a veil of suicide.

And so I was able to say, "My brother took his own life," as I witnessed in front of six hundred people in October 1986. The pastor of Medjugorje, Dr. Fr. Tomislav Pervan, OFM, was at our Mass in New York, and that filled me with a certainty that the Holy Spirit was indeed working in my life. The scriptures became more real to me as I read what St. Paul wrote to the Corinthians. *"We have not received the spirit of the world but the Spirit that is from God, so that we may understand the things freely given us by God."* (1 Cor. 2:12) The gift of courage from the Holy Spirit, along with Our Lady's grace of compassion and understanding, helped me to listen with love to others and not to be afraid to give of myself. *"Give and gifts will be given to you; a good measure packed together, shaken down, and overflowing, will be poured into your lap. For the measure with which you measure will in return be measured out to you."* (Lk 6:38)

When someone comes to me after a talk and expresses sadness at losing someone special to them, my heart reaches out to that person, not as a stranger, but as someone who is much loved by God. We are both covered by Our Lady's mantle, and I pray I am able to help this person see the light of Christ through that suffering.

Our Lady's message of March 25, 1988, continually helps me in my desire to give Chucky back to God. She says: **"Dear Children! Today also I am inviting you to a complete surrender to God. Dear children, you are not conscious of how God loves you with such a great love because He permits me to be with you so I can instruct you and help you to find the way of peace. This way, however, you cannot discover if you do not pray. Therefore, dear children, forsake everything and consecrate your time to God and God will bestow gifts upon you and bless you. Little children, don't forget that your life is fleeting like a spring flower which today is wondrously beautiful but tomorrow has vanished. Therefore, pray in such a way that your prayer, your surrender to God, may become like a road sign. That way, your witness will not only have value for yourselves but for all eternity. Thank you for having responded to my call."**

I sincerely thank Our Blessed Lord for taking Chucky before He took me because it is a direct result of my brother's death that I have discovered our true Mother. Through Mary, I have come to know, love, and follow Jesus, and through Chucky I have followed the road signs to know, love, and follow Mary.

The peace and love of God that I discovered are gifts that Our Lady wanted me to share. In Christ's words, *"Let the children come to me and do not prevent them; for the kingdom of God belongs to such as these"* (Lk 18:16), were brought into our living room soon after my conversion, by a special group of teens who filled our home with inexpressible joy and never ending surprises.

Chapter Eleven

Teens Together

"Dear Children! Today, I am calling you to pray. Dear Children, you are forgetting that you are all important. The elderly are especially important in the family. Urge them to pray. Let the young people be an example to the others. Let them be a witness to Jesus by their lives." (Taken from Our Lady's messages at Medjugorje, April 24, 1984)

The peace and love of God that I discovered are gifts that Our Lady wanted me to share. Christ's words, *"Let the children come to me and do not prevent them; for the kingdom of God belongs to such as these"* (Lk 18:16), were brought into our living room soon after my conversion by a special group of teens who filled our home with inexpressible joy and never ending surprises.

Throughout the summer of 1985, many of the rosaries my children and I said together were prayed outside in our yard. I tried to be true to my promise of asking for a family rosary two nights a week, and I didn't receive much opposition. The opportunity to introduce the rosary to our children's friends was there without having to be contrived.

The invitation was extended to all. I know it was only through a grace from Our Lady that my daughter Lori's friends, all fourteen and fifteen years old, joined us.

Most of the time, reverence was absent, so I just closed my eyes and tried not to be disturbed by their childish play. At first, I became uptight and thought to myself, "Are they being disrespectful?" Then, I realized that at least they were praying while they were playing. I pulled in the reigns every now and then as was needed, but, little by little, some were getting serious about it. Even Chad began to settle down and saved his push-ups until after the rosary.

I was learning the importance of giving praise and thanks to God at this time through my prayer group, and it was a perfect opportunity to introduce this to the children. After we finished our rosary, we would go around in a circle and give praise and thanks to God for two special graces in our lives. Most of the time, one would repeat after the other, "I praise and thank you, Lord, for my friends and family." After months of their all too familiar praise, one by one, they began to add different reflections for which they were grateful. We were taken by surprise when the least serious of all the children present one night suddenly thanked God for his life. He had been struck by a train just a year before. It was his witness in giving glory to God that helped us thank Our Lord for all the miracles in our lives, both big and small.

I was surprised at how two of the boys, John and Scott, would suddenly appear at our door to call for Lori and, if she wasn't at home, would stay and talk for quite some time. No matter what I was doing, being totally present to them was important. Our conversations gave me some insight into the problems of teens in the 1980's, problems which would soon be up and coming in my own family. An unanticipated sense of caring about what these boys were experiencing began to take hold of my heart. I looked forward to their visits which were filled with joy and laughter. Not only did we talk about their problems, but they helped me to become sensitive to my own children's needs. A bond of trust and respect for one another's opinions was growing.

At this time, I was still in awe of how much Jesus and Mary loved us, and I wanted more than anything to share their love. I knew how easy it could be to turn someone off unintentionally, and so I prayed each evening for Our Lady to clear the path to help me express how special they and their problems were to her Son. It was years since they had gone to church, and that was all the more reason they needed to know how much God loved them. I told them that the fact that they were praying the rosary didn't just happen out of nowhere. *"It was not you who chose me, but I who chose you."* (Jn. 15:16)

One afternoon, I was going to confession and out of a clear blue sky I asked John, Scott, and two others if they wanted to join me. I didn't have to ask twice. On our way, we talked about different anxieties we each felt in going to confession. Scott was quiet. He entered the confessional before I did. I suddenly realized that I didn't even know if Scott was Catholic. When he came out, he said, *Father wants to talk to you.* My knees buckled. I went into the confessional apologizing for putting Father in an awkward position since Scott had not been to confession since his First Holy Communion. Immediately, Father responded, *I don't know what you're doing, but don't apologize for it. They all think the world of you, and you seem to be a very good influence on them.* I was on Cloud Nine, and my ego started to soar. Remembering Our Lady's words: **"Live the messages I am giving you in humbleness,"** helped me to stop and realize, it wasn't me, but *"The love of God has been poured out into our hearts through the Holy Spirit that has been given to us."* (Rom. 5:5)

My prayer partner suggested that since these kids were coming to pray and opening up about God, I should do something with them. He encouraged me to try to get something together. When I shared this with another friend, he cautioned me about taking a big risk. He didn't have to remind me that I had no credentials for teaching religious education. I almost gave up my dream. Then he read to me from the Bible: *"Whoever causes one of these little ones who believe in me to sin, it would be better for him to have a great millstone hung around his neck and to be downed in the depths of the sea."* (Mt 18:6) I understood what he was trying to tell me. He suggested that I call my parish and seek their guidance to keep this group under the umbrella of the

Church. That brought to light Our Lady's message: **"Dear Children! Today I want to call you to work in the Church. I love all the same and I desire from each one to work as much as is possible. I know, dear children, that you can, but you do not wish to because you feel small and humble in these things. You need to be courageous and with little flowers do your share for the church and for Jesus so that everyone can be satisfied. Thank you for having responded to my call."** (October 31, 1985)

At this time, I had been going to daily Mass for almost two years, but that was my only involvement in my parish. I didn't know any of our priests personally and, until I remembered Our Lady's message, I was very content to leave it that way. Mary was right. I didn't feel worthy. Once again, I was called to trust. *"In all your ways be mindful of him, and he will make straight your path."* (Prv 3:6)

Our Lady has said from Medjugorje: **"I wish to guide you and show you the joy which I want to bring to all of you."** Our Lady's guidance brought me to pray on Sunday nights with our parish deacon to discern what it was that the Lord wanted. It was a struggle to give up my favorite night of the week at home, and I felt inadequate praying with someone with a great gift of prayer and who I'd always held in great esteem. This deacon taught me patience and endurance and that everything requires prayer. My impetuous nature was toned down during this time of waiting and praying. *"You need endurance to do the will of God and re-*

ceive what he has promised." (Heb. 10:36) Before I knew it, Sunday nights were mine again. I received the Church's blessing to meet with the teens on Tuesday evenings from our deacon and our parish priest, both of whom said they would be there if we needed them. *"I know your works, behold, I have left an open door before you, which no one can close."* (Rev. 3:8)

Each teen who joined our group had a special story to tell. I treasure the many experiences that brought me so much closer to God through them. The trials and errors experienced as we first established our purpose for being together were difficult, but necessary.

From the very beginning, I felt that this group would be dedicated to Our Lady. This was confirmed as I listened to a talk by Fr. Slavko Barbaric in Medjugorje: "To those who wish to organize prayer groups: consecrate yourselves totally to Our Lady, and I guarantee that she will be in your midst and will guide you in an interior way. Our Lady is truly present whenever there is true opening of the heart, and she guides every group and person." Fr. Barbaric, became involved in the events at Medjugorje in 1983, when Bishop Zanic of Mostar, the local diocese, wanted to discover if the visions were authentic. He asked Fr. Slavko, a trained psychotherapist, to investigate. After many interviews with the visionaries and lengthy investigations, Fr. Slavko came to believe in the visions himself. Fr. Slavko undoubtedly was instrumental in organizing the three-hour prayer program in Medjugorje as he was appointed to the parish of St. James in 1984.

Our Lady's message established a format that pleased everyone, as long as it didn't take more than fifteen minutes of our hour and a half together. Her message on June 12, 1986 was: **"Dear Children! Today I am calling you to begin to pray the rosary with a living faith. That way I will be able to help you. You, dear children, want to obtain graces, but you do not want to get started. Dear children, I am calling you to pray the rosary and that your rosary be an obligation which you shall fulfill with joy. That way you shall understand the reason I am with you this long. I desire to teach you to pray. Thank you for having responded to my call."**

The teens valued the rosaries that were given to them and blessed by Our Lady. I was so surprised at how they took to heart a teaching that I had learned from a priest in my parish just weeks before. As he was blessing the rosaries belonging to my two nephews, he said, "Boys, even if you don't use them, keep them in your pocket. That in itself is an act of faith and a prayer." I laugh as I think of what happened to one of the boys in our group. He and some of his friends were taken to a local police station and held for their parents to come and get them because one of them was carrying a knife. He said that, as the officers came to him to empty his pockets, they couldn't believe that he had a knife in one pocket and a rosary in the other.

Our Lady's message of July 18, 1985, reads: **"Dear Children! Today I call you to place more blessed objects in your homes and that everyone put some blessed objects on their person. Bless all the objects and thus Satan will attack you less because you will have armor against him. Thank you for having responded to my call."** This made me more aware of the importance of holy water as a means of spiritual protection. The children and I all believe that the devil hates holy water because of its power over him.

He cannot abide long in a place or near a person that is often sprinkled with blessed water. God is so good and patient in His ways of teaching; the importance of using sacramentals in the home, such as blessed candles and holy water, should have been in my home long ago. Our Lady reminds us of their value, and I thank God that it's never too late to learn. One of my greatest joys was learning, along with a wonderful group of young people, all Our Lady was teaching us. We began our meetings by liberally blessing the room with holy water, then acknowledging its great power over Satan, whom we knew was very unhappy about a group of ten to twenty praying teenagers.

After our rosary, we would interact for some time on different matters of faith and try to incorporate these lessons into our own everyday lives. Sometimes, I would get discouraged because many of our discussions would end up as a joke and there would be no way I could steer them towards more serious matters. On the other hand, we had exchanges that had a tremendous rippling effect on each of us. One girl witnessed what she went through as her mom suffered from alcoholism. She told us how she felt not knowing what her mom was going to be like from one day to the next. Her responsibilities at home became overwhelming as she tried to cover up for her mom's drinking. Our hearts ached for her when she filled with tears and tried to express how she wished her mom had not died and, at the same time, resented that she hadn't helped herself. The beginning of a healing was taking place as she realized towards the end of the evening that she needed to forgive her mother. In one way or another, there wasn't one among us who couldn't identify with her pain and also with the difficult task ahead of her. *"A time to weep, and a time to laugh; a time to mourn, and a time to dance."* (Eccl 3:1)

When the father of a young boy named John was diagnosed with cancer, it brought forth an unparalleled sense of love and compassion that I would not have imagined possible from a group of teens. One of the fellows suggested that, instead of a regular prayer meeting, we would go and visit John's father at home. This night in particular, the girls in the group were not able to come for one reason or another. John asked his dad if he would mind if the rest of the group came. He welcomed us. As we picked up a pizza and soda to bring to his house, I said to the boys, "I've never met John's father before and most of you guys know him for a long time. Why don't I drop you off and I'll pick you up around nine?"

They laughed saying, "Come on, Mrs. A., you've got to come." I felt like a mother hen with her chicks, except they all towered over me. I was so proud of them since this was their own idea. I knew this visit wouldn't be easy. I should not have been surprised when they disappeared to watch the ball game after eating, and I ended up talking with John's father for over an hour. That evening taught me a great lesson through Our Lady's message of June 20, 1985: **"Open your hearts to the Master of all hearts. Give me all your feelings and all your problems! I wish to comfort you in all your trials. I wish to fill you with peace, joy, and love of God. Thank you for having responded to my call."**

The fear I had of not knowing what to expect, or what I was going to say to John's father, helped me to surrender my anxieties to Our Lady. That evening, the peace and love of God filled all of our hearts with a memory we'll never forget. *"Happy are those whose greatest desire is to do what God requires; God will satisfy them fully!"* (Mt 5:6) Eventually, John would come to visit during his lunch break at school. He confided how hard it was to watch his dad suffer. His gift of tears was a beautiful display of just how much he loved his father. He wasn't sure if there was a God; for, certainly, if He heard all of our prayers, this wouldn't be happening. His love was so deep that he begged God to let him take on all of his father's pain. He was angry with me as I pleaded with him to listen to a tape I had on the meaning of suffering. But it was not a tape on suffering that John needed. What he needed was ears to listen, arms to hug him, and love to comfort him.

After John's father died, he called and said there was just no way could he come back to the meetings. I tried not to panic when he said he would never pray again, for I knew he needed time. One Tuesday night as we went to visit the nursing home instead of a meeting, John asked if I would pick him up on our way. When we started to pray a decade of the rosary, John made a motion to get out of the car, but he didn't follow through. I prayed with all my heart that Jesus and Mary would help John realize their love for him. On the way home, the kids were praying the decades at random. My heart skipped a beat when John said a Hail Mary right before we pulled up to his house. John knew he was never alone in his grief, as the others in the group would continuously soak him in love and rally around him. *"Bear one another's burdens, and so you will fulfill the law of Christ."* (Gal 6:2)

In God's time, not mine, the group's understanding of what we are called to do as Christians began to seep into their consciousness. Around Thanksgiving, they put the Gospel into action. *"Each one should give, then, as he has decided, not with regret or out of a sense of duty; for God loves the one who gives gladly."* (2 Cor. 9:7) They talked about who could use our small help at this special time of year. One of the boys suggested a friend of ours named Gladys. Gladys was in her twenties and confined to a wheelchair. It takes a lot of patience to understand her speech. She lived with her family in an extremely poor neighborhood. The group decided to contribute five dollars each and, totally on their own, they shopped for groceries for a Thanksgiving dinner. I'll never forget the expression on their faces as they helped put away the groceries with her mom. The cupboards were bare and, although I had forewarned them what to expect, it still took them by surprise. Before our visit was over, I asked Gladys if she wanted to pray with us. She was so proud of every syllable as she struggled to maintain our pace. On our way home, the group's conversation of how blessed they were, helped me to realize how blessed I was, as I saw Christ tending to the needs of the poor and the handicapped in each and every one of them.

When the group first began, my husband, Mike, was open to having the meetings at our house, though warning me: "Just don't get me involved!" Throughout the years, I saw how much he gave of himself to these teens without even realizing it. If the teens were without cars, and Mike wasn't working, he'd drive them home. At first, everyone lived locally, but as time progressed, there were a few who joined our group who lived a good distance away. God's way of gently establishing a rapport between Mike and each of the kids, whether it was through driving them home or their common interest in golf or music, became an absolute blessing.

Our Lady confirmed to me how much both Mike and I were necessary to make this group work when she showed

me how Mike helped them in a situation in which I felt helpless. It was an afternoon I'll never forget. Four of the boys in
our group sat in our living room with broken hearts because
the night before one of their classmates had tried to commit
suicide. It wasn't only the fact that we were both there for
them at this critical time, but it was Mike's gift of talking to
these young men to be grateful their classmate was still alive
that helped lift the boys' spirits.

Recently, the group had been talking about how they all
started coming one by one to the meetings. Though I was
embarrassed, I laughed as Mark said, "Mrs. A., I don't want
to insult you, but when I first met you, I thought you were a
lunatic. Then when I met Mr. A., I said, "There is no way I'll
go near him." I'd tried to forget that night, but I knew exactly
what Mark was talking about. It seemed like yesterday. It was
around the time when two teenage girls living in our vicinity
were missing for some time and on that particular day one
of the girls was found slain. That evening there was a group
of youths I didn't know personally, Mark among them, in the
field near our house. They were friends of a neighbor, and
my Lori was with them. When it was time for Lori to come
in, no one knew where she was. I panicked. Right away, my
trust in God flew right out the window. When I saw her
approaching our corner ten minutes later, I flew out the door
to bring her in. I was screaming and yelling at her, really
creating a scene. The fear of her being kidnapped was all I
could think of. We laugh today as they jokingly tell of their

first impression of me. I wish it weren't one of their fondest memories, but then again, God is the potter, and I am the clay. With me, He can mold forever!

When the group started forming, I prayed with all of my heart that Lori would join us. But she had to come in her own time though I tried to bribe her a few times. It hurt me sometimes. She was happy to see everybody as they came in, but once the meeting started, she went off to her room until the end of the meeting. I was so proud of her when she joined us to visit Gladys. She understood what Gladys was saying better than anyone in the room, including me. I prayed that maybe now she would be a part of the group, but it was just a dream. The following week, we were back to square one.

I recalled a gift that Our Lady blessed me with on the mountain in Medjugorje, and so I asked for the same treasure in reference to Lori. The first time was in December of 1985. I prayed at Mt. Krizevac for two boys in our area who would sit outside our house on Tuesday nights and make fun of their friends who were coming to the meetings. I brought them in my heart to Our Lady on the mountain and prayed that they would be moved at least to come in and see what we were all about. Within a month of my return, these two boys were the most faithful in coming to our meetings. Although not every week, Lori began joining our group, and it was a sure sign in my life that God does answer our prayers. *"Your Father knows what you need before you ask Him."* (Mt 6:8)

Our favorite part of the meetings was when we would turn off all the lights and sit by a blessed candle. We would pray to the Holy Spirit to help settle us down. Our Lady has said: **"I want to say to the young especially: be open to the Holy Spirit because God wants to draw you to Himself."** (May 16, 1985) The petitions expressed by these youths often put me to shame. They poured out their hearts and souls. I learned how to pray from one of our girls, Mary, who started off by saying, "Hi, God, it's me again. It's been a tough week for me." Mary would then converse with God as though it were just the two of them in the room. If there was a giggle here or there, Mary was filled with the grace to ignore it.

Another time, one of our group leaders, Tom, included in his petition, "For all the souls in Purgatory, we pray to The Lord." Tom is Lutheran, and I couldn't believe my ears. When I questioned his belief in Purgatory, Tom responded, "Well, I never thought of it before until you started praying for them, but why not?" It was Our Lady's message of November 6, 1986, that had made an impact on them. **"Dear Children! Today I call you to pray daily for the souls in Purgatory. For every soul prayer and grace is necessary to reach God and the love of God. By doing this, dear children, you obtain new intercessors who will help you in life to realize that all the earthly things are not important for you, that only Heaven is that for which it is necessary to strive. Therefore, dear children, pray without ceasing that you may be able to help yourselves and the others to whom**

your prayers will bring joy. Thank you for having responded to my call." Tom's prayers, I'm sure, were what motivated the others in the group to remember the souls in Purgatory.

There wasn't a week that went by without Mark including Mr. Jones in his prayers. (I wrote about Mr. Jones who died of cancer in Chapter 4.) Mark had never met Mr. Jones, but from my witness, the Holy Spirit must have placed him in Mark's heart to pray. It was funny one night when towards the end of our prayers of petition, it was Paul who included Mr. Jones in his prayers. He and Mark began to argue over who was to pray for him. Mary's messages were undoubtedly beginning to come alive. **"Dear children: I am inviting you so that your prayer may be a joyful encounter with the Lord. I cannot guide you unless you yourself experience joy in prayer. I want to guide you in prayer more and more, from day to day, but I do not want to force you."** (August 14, 1986) The joy these teens brought into our house every week came through the rosary, our link to Jesus.

Our Lady's words to the seers in Medjugorje: **"I do not want to force you,"** is a gentle reminder to allow each and every member of a group to meet Our Blessed Lord when he or she is ready. I've had to surrender the disappointment which I've experienced knowing that at least eighty percent of the group doesn't go to Mass. I have finally realized they've got to come when they're ready, not when I think they're ready. The grace of God flows through them, and it's only a matter of time before they really realize the priceless gift God offers them through the sacraments.

During Holy Week, I prayed and asked others to join me in prayer for the group to experience the grace of reconciliation. I didn't push the issue, but with Father Bill as our spiritual coordinator, they were enthusiastically encouraged. With fifteen of us in the rectory's sitting room, I suggested we pray a rosary for one another. That was all that was necessary. The power of their Hail Marys encouraged one fellow to go to confession after five years. He beamed as we drove home. He commented, "It wasn't as bad as I thought it would be. I guess all those Hail Marys I've been saying are working." When he told me the following Tuesday that he didn't have a chance to go to Mass on Easter because there was too much to do, I was disappointed, but not ready to give up. The love that Our Lord has for that boy filled my heart as I said, "At least you made the first step by going to confession." *"Whatever happens or can happen has already happened before. God makes the same thing happen again and again."* (Eccl 3:15) Through the grace of Our Lady, the opportunity for him to go to confession will always happen again. Perhaps next time it will be followed with a desire to receive Our Lord in the Eucharist.

It was the belief these teens were being blessed that prompted me to step out in faith so many times, which I could have never done before. For example, one day Karen called to ask for prayers for her dad because she was very concerned for her dad who was on his way to the hospital for an x-ray. She shared with me that before he had left, she gave him some rosary beads and a scapular. I was so proud of Karen for giving her dad these signs of her faith as she placed her love and trust in Our Lady's intercession.

I thank Jesus and Mary for the opportunity to share this book because through it, I realize how much I cherished these teens at the time, and still do. They know me better than some of my closest friends. When I am feeling low, it seems as if the Lord knows just how to raise my spirits with one of their impromptu visits. As Gina always prayed when the lights went off, "I'd like to thank God for this prayer group and for Penny," I say in the depths of my heart, "Oh, if they only knew! If they only knew it's not I, but Our Lady, who is responsible for them being here." They thank me for all I've given them, but I'm the one who received so much through them. *"Whoever receives in my name one such child as this, receives me."* (Mt 18:5) Together we laughed, we cried, we loved, and we leaned. When I close my eyes, I can imagine Our Lady with her arms around us on a Tuesday night saying, "Dear children, we've only just begun."

Chapter Twelve

Through the Years

"Do not ignore this one fact, beloved, that with the Lord one day is like a thousand years and a thousand years like one day." (2 Peter 3:8) Since I was reintroduced to Our Lady through the rosary, the years that have passed seem like yesterday. I first walked into the church of St. James in 1984. Now, as of this writing (August 2019), I look forward to my 103rd pilgrimage this October, like it is my first. I love to reflect back on my early years in Medjugorje, and I thank Our Lord and Our Lady for this soft-hued time to reflect on some beautiful memories of years past.

I treasure the lessons I learned in Medjugorje as I discovered the real presence of God. Upon returning from this holy ground, several people shared that they had witnessed the miracle of the sun. They said it was possible for them to look into the sun for as long as twenty minutes without hurting their eyes. I felt very peaceful in telling them that I believed them, yet I didn't know if that gift was for everyone, including myself. *"Have you come to believe because you have seen me? Blessed are those who have not seen and have believed."* (Jn. 20:29)

But on the feast day of the Immaculate Conception, December 8, 1985, I too received the special grace to see the beauty of this solar phenomenon. While I was praying on Mt. Krizevac, I looked up at the sky a few moments before 3 p.m. and saw nothing more than the bright sun. Then I looked again, and I saw the sun quite clearly. It seemed as if a disc was within the perimeter of the sun but somewhat smaller than the sun. *The disc looked like a communion host.* It was breathtaking as I watched it spin rapidly in a clockwise direction. Brilliant colors of gold and crimson emitted around the sun's perimeter, and it seemed to pulsate like a beating heart. *"For God has shone in our hearts, that we in turn might make known the glory of God."* (2 Cor. 4:6) The gift of that miracle for me was a lesson in praising and thanking God. The following day in the courtyard of St. James, I again witnessed the spinning of the sun. Without hesitation, I went into church to pray. I knew the miracle of the sun was the glory of God, yet the real presence of God was not in the sun, but in the Blessed Sacrament.

Reports show that many pilgrims who have been to Medjugorje are blessed with physical healings. My friend, Tom, was one of those most fortunate. On this particular pilgrimage in 1985, Tom was among several friends that journeyed with me to Medjugorje. He was a member of my prayer group at Molloy College and, although twenty years older than I, his determination to go to Medjugorje was un-wavering. Our first day in the village, we unexpectedly met the visionary, Marija Pavlovic, praying with a group of pilgrims. Tom was the last one to leave the courtyard as Marija wished him God's blessing. Climbing the small mountain immediately afterwards, Tom seemed to have lost his footing. It wasn't that at all. Tom was experiencing his fifth heart attack. He was able to throw down his jacket first before falling on it and losing consciousness.

We did what we felt Our Lady would have told us to do – "Pray, pray, pray." Our prayers seemed to be answered immediately. Within minutes of his attack, Our Blessed Lord provided a nurse who was coming down from the mountain, and then a priest who gave Tom, what was called in 1985, the last rites. Twenty minutes later, Tom felt strong enough to rise to his feet. He was determined to go down the hill on his own. What amazed Tom most about his fall was the fact that the rocks on which he had rested were full of mud from the morning rain, yet his jacket didn't have a speck of dirt on it. It seemed as if the angels had cushioned his fall.

Tom would not give in to his heart attack. Obstinately, he refused to go back to the house where we were staying to rest before the evening service in Church. That meant standing for three hours from 5 p.m. until 8. Throughout our stay, he kept a pace that most of us had difficulty keeping up with. Not only did we witness the power of Our Divine Healer restore Tom's exhausted heart, but six days later he climbed up 1,400 feet to the top of Mt. Krizevac and gave thanks to God for his new life. During Holy Communion, when Fr.

Bob Fericy said, *"This is the body of Christ,"* Tom responded with unyielding conviction, *"I believe!"*

Our Lady has said on December 18, 1986: **"Dear Children! Once again I desire to call you to prayer. When you pray you are much more beautiful like flowers, which after the snow, show all their beauty and all the colors become indescribable. So also you, dear children, after prayer show before God all so much more what is beautiful and are beloved by Him. Therefore, dear children, pray and open your inner self to the Lord so that He makes of you a harmonious and beautiful flower for Paradise. Thank you for having responded to my call."**

One of my pilgrims from the mid-80's was a beautiful young girl named Ann, who was a guest of her Aunt's generosity. Within days of our pilgrimage, Ann received a very special grace of realizing God's tremendous love for her. She appeared to me to be that flower Our Lady spoke of after the snow. We became friendly as we often, unexpectedly, found ourselves in each other's paths during our pilgrimage. Her Croatian heritage motivated her desire to fully experience life in this Croatian village. Walking home from church in the afternoons, I would see Ann feeding the chickens, tending sheep, or even watching a hog being slaughtered. Her love for her way of life filled her with joy, yet, in my heart, I felt there was more to Ann than feeding chickens. Two days before Ann was to leave for home, we had a very moving conversation about the spiritual awareness we'd each experienced. I prayed that Our Lady would bring us together again.

To my surprise and delight, Ann visited me the night before she was to leave. We talked about the Blessed Mother in our lives. And then I found the courage to ask her if she prayed the rosary. Her fragile silence was a beautiful opening for me to describe how precious the rosary was in my life. That very afternoon, I had been given a special rosary from a local priest, which I immediately adopted as my favorite. I suddenly realized that it wasn't for me, but for Ann. She held the rosary tightly while we spoke of Our Lady's message of prayer and reconciliation. The Holy Spirit filled Ann's heart with the desire to go to confession before she left the next morning. We wondered where we'd find an English-speaking priest to hear confession at 8 a.m. *"Whatever you ask for in prayer with faith, you will receive."* (Mt 21:22)

The next morning, Ann and I met at the top of the hill to walk down to church. Showers of graces, in the form of precipitation, soaked us to the bone. We were both so excited that we hardly felt the rain. Ann told me she'd slept with the rosary in her hand. She couldn't believe the peace and security it brought her. I knew exactly what she was saying. Holding my rosary is like holding Our Lady's hand.

When we walked into church, I was surprised that it was empty. I thought at least the Blessed Mother would have had a priest here waiting for us. Two minutes later, I knocked at the parish house and asked if an English-speaking priest was available. "Not at this time," was the response, and my heart sank. Suddenly, the library door opened, and the priest who had said our Mass in English the day before was in front of me. I asked if it were convenient for him to hear confession, and within minutes he was over in the church sitting with Ann.

She absolutely radiated during Mass despite the black under her eyes from her smudged make-up and rain-saturated hair and clothing. I felt blessed praying alongside Father as we petitioned the heavens for her safe flight home. While praying in the silence of my heart, I felt how precious Ann was to Our Lord. I thanked Our Lady for allowing me to see the exquisite beauty of opening someone's inner self to the Lord.

Before I returned home from this trip in December 1985, I wrote a note to Our Lady. I asked if I could come back again, but this time, with a priest. I had no idea when that would be. I simply knew in my heart how important it was for Our Lord's priests to witness the testimonies of faith, penance, prayer, and conversion that pour forth from this remote village. I had been witnessing to different groups at this time, but I felt Our Lady's message would have more of an impact coming from a priest. I had no particular priest in mind. I asked that it be Our Lady's choice. Our Lady must have read my note because the next time I returned to Medjugorje, and every time since, we have had a priest with us. *"If you remain in me and my words remain in you, ask for whatever you want and it will be done for you."* (Jn. 15:7)

A particular journey in February of 1986 was entrusted to St. Michael the Archangel to protect us from the beginning to the end. We received a special blessing from Our Lady on the Hill of the Cross, or Mt. Krizevac as it is traditionally known. It was our last night in Medjugorje. Mary told the visionaries during the apparition in the parish house that she would meet them on Mt. Krizevac at 10:30 that evening. Marija and Ivan led the prayer group of about thirty youth up the mountain. They climbed in total darkness, praying the rosary and making the Stations of the Cross. Our Lady would meet with the children twice in one day many times throughout the years, and this evening the pilgrims had been invited. It was a beautiful, clear, but very cold night. When we reached the top of the hill, I was mesmerized by the true sense of holiness that filled these young adults as they sang songs of devotion and praise to the heavens for nearly an hour. I thought, "Oh, what love!" Suddenly, there was a hush! I looked up in the sky and saw a shooting star. Then a flash, out of nowhere, seemed to light up the cross beam of the huge stone cross. I knew at that moment that something very special was about to happen. Although there were over one hundred people present on the mountain, Our Lady appeared only to Marija and Ivan, as she did in the apparition room. They say she is preceded by a ray of light like no other. A perfect quiet filled the winter air as the visionaries communicated with the Mother of God.

The apparition lasted nearly five minutes, and it was immediately translated into four different languages by a villager who was very close to the visionaries. Marija said, "Our Lady appeared with five angels, and she was very joyful. Our Lady thanked all of us for being part of a special plan which Our Lord was fulfilling." Marija continued, "Blessed Mother said she will give all of us the strength and courage to continue to pray." And *those* are the words I rely upon so often. Whenever I find it difficult to pray, I know not to give up because Mary has promised us the strength and courage to continue to pray.

Months later, during another pilgrimage, on the evening of August 21, 1986, I was at Mass in St. James as Mary's message was read from the altar. **"Dear Children! I thank you for the love which you are showing me. You know, dear children, that I love you immeasurably and daily I pray the Lord to help you to understand the love which I am showing you. Therefore, you dear children, pray, pray, pray."**

With her words, I was humbly reminded of the personal struggles I encountered on this particular trip. To be sincere in saying, *"Teach me, O Lord, your way that I may walk in your truth."* (Ps. 86:11) was an absolute challenge. Instead of looking to Our Lady in the hardships that she and St. Joseph experienced on their way to Bethlehem, I was busy complaining about everything, in particular, the 100-degree temperatures.

I thought of Jesus being born in a stable. Here was a tiny infant, the Son of God, exposed to elements beyond my comprehension, and I was feeling sorry for myself. When I finally realized I should be counting my blessings, Our Lady helped me understand the love she was showing me.

Being in Medjugorje in the warmer weather filled my heart with an anticipation of Our Lady's appearance that I can never forget. In church, before apparition time, the sounds of the birds filled the air outside. Hundreds of them perched in trees surrounding the church and the parish house. It seemed they knew the Mother of God would soon appear. Late one afternoon, as I approached St. James, there wasn't a bird in sight. Suddenly, the air was filled with them, flying from every direction, preparing their harmonious song for Our Lady's visit. Most amazing was that the birds could be heard singing until the time of the Eucharist. And then, a pious quiet prevailed.

Our entire stay that August, 1986, was filled with never-ending surprises. I traveled this journey with a priest whose great love for Our Lady had inspired me tremendously. With us was Mary, from our teenage prayer group, and Kathleen, whose gift of music brought young and old from many nations together in song. The Holy Spirit prompted our conversations each evening and then confirmed them the next day at Mass.

One night we were talking about Our Lady's message to pray constantly and the challenge it presents to be faithful in setting aside prayer time each day. I was fascinated by a homily the next morning given by a Benedictine Monk about prayer. He shared that when people ask him how much to pray, he simply told them to double what they presently do. He explained, "If you pray two minutes a day, pray four minutes. Then when you're comfortable with four minutes each day, double it. Then double it again." He added, "Every time we double our prayers to Our Lord, the graces that we receive are doubled. So, it really depends on us, how much we wish to receive." *"Consider this: whoever sows sparingly will also reap sparingly, and whoever sows bountifully will also reap bountifully."* (2 Cor 9:6) On November 8, 1984, Our Lady said through the visionary, Marija, **"If you knew the gifts God is offering you, you would pray continuously!"**

Our Lady has repeated numerous times in her messages: **"I am calling you to prayer and complete surrender to God."** If I could have followed her direction just recently, I would have saved myself a lot of anxiety.

In March of 1987, six months since my last trip to Medjugorje, I missed the village and the family with whom I stayed. My husband Mike was unbelievably supportive and said that it would be no problem if I wanted to go back. In fact, he encouraged me to go. I asked my spiritual director's opinion about making plans, fully knowing that, if I was to be obedient to my spiritual director, I couldn't pick and choose when his direction suited me. He advised that the trip was up to me, but he felt that my first priority was to be at home with my family.

My childish personality emerged causing me to not trust that Father's direction. I found myself silently pouting. My disappointment created internal confusion. After two days of not being able to accept God's will, my friend, Cathy, encouraged me to surrender my disappointment to Our Lord. She told me, "When you do, wait until you see what happens."

At Mass the following morning, during the Consecration as the priest raised the host, I prayed for the grace to lift all my feelings to Our Lord. *"To you I lift up my soul, O Lord, my God."* (Ps. 25:1-2) Seven hours later, I was asked to go to Medjugorje as a spiritual guide with a group from Nashville, Tennessee, and all the doors were opened wide. Mike and the children joined me in my enthusiasm, and Father said, "Yes, you should go." He said, "Don't you realize that now you're being called?" Oh, if I only could have listened to Our Lady from the beginning. **"I call you to prayer and to surrender to God."**

When my feet touched the ground again, my nervousness settled in, and I began to panic. What did I know about taking a group on a pilgrimage? I'd always been pretty selfish in sharing Medjugorje with three or four friends. Yet, Our Lady must have had other plans. Now there were eighty of us. When I said to my trusted friend, Sr. Mildred, "What do

I do?" she simply said, "Penny, be yourself. Our Lady will take care of the rest."

All my anxieties began to fade when I met the group at the airport. I received an exceptional grace to relax in their love. They were a very special group, mostly from one parish, who seemed to have come together to pray for little Mary Margaret who had cystic fibrosis. You would never know that Mary Margaret, only nine months old, was sick. She was bathed in love by her family, friends, and fellow parishioners; it was something to behold.

Our Lady abundantly blessed the group from Nashville on that pilgrimage, and she also blessed me. The families from Nashville stayed in guest houses near apparition hill. For myself, I appeared unexpectedly on the doorstep of the family that I usually stayed with and was welcomed with open arms. Staying at the same house were two priests from Ireland, and their support was priceless. If someone in our group asked a question that I wasn't qualified to answer, the priests spent time with me to help me feel confident in my reply. We prayed the rosary together each night with our host family. I felt in my heart that Our Lady had reserved my place there and that she could count on the two priests to help me out. To me, that is what Medjugorje is all about. Our Lady brings her children together to help one another.

I have also been blessed to witness a before-and-after situation. This aided me in realizing how Our Lady needs us to be there for one another. When I first traveled to Medjugorje with John and David in 1984, the village was empty compared to the countless visitors of today. Years ago, there was a good possibility of spending quiet time with a religious sister or priest. Today, that is almost impossible. The demands on priests and sisters have increased as the number of pilgrims from all over the world grows into the millions. The vast responsibilities of priests and sisters exhaust what little spare time they have. The same holds true with the visionaries. My heart reaches out to them. Anyone can see that their time and privacy have been sacrificed for their love of Jesus and Mary. Amazingly, their smiles, peacefulness, and patience never seem to leave them.

I thanked God that meeting the visionaries or the need to be present during an apparition was not a priority for the group from Nashville. The reason for their pilgrimage was to pray, and that's exactly the path Our Lady led us on. Our Lady provided time to be alone with the Lord, and other times in which Mary would guide us to pray together.

Our Lady took us to Calvary through our ascent to the top of Mt. Krizevac. The beautiful displays of one person helping another to accomplish the rugged climb symbolized Our Lady always being there for us through others.

One couple from our group opened my eyes to the virtue of charity by putting into action the words of scripture: *"Whoever has two cloaks should share with the person who has none."* (Lk 3:11) They did this without a second thought to a group we met from Zimbabwe, South Africa, who were truly in need of warmer clothing.

How worried I was about helping to lead a large group! Our Lady planted all the seeds. My job was simply to water them. One example of this was when our tour guide suggested to the group that we go to Confession before evening Mass. Our Lady provided three priests to hear confessions. For many, that was the true beginning of their spiritual climb to Mt. Tabor. As I thanked one of the Fathers for the three hours he spent hearing confessions, he told me it was a gift for him to be there. "They were beautiful moments," he added.

The members of the group, which, surprisingly, consisted of quite a few complete families, were all so patient with me. As we walked up the Hill of Apparitions, someone suggested we pray a rosary. The unity of that rosary paved our way to feel comfortable enough to pray together whenever and wherever we were. Even the twelve young adults, who ranged in age from eleven to seventeen, joined us in prayer, shining brighter than we, their role models.

Imagining youngsters going to Mass every day for three hours seems beyond comprehension yet, that's what they did. They became perfect examples of Our Lady's message of May 16, 1985: **"Dear Children! I am calling you to more attentive prayer and participation in the Mass. I want your Mass to be an experience of God. I want to say to the young especially: Be open to the Holy Spirit because God wants**

to draw you to Himself these days when Satan is active." The last two days of our trip, I was blessed by being able to spend quite a bit of time with the youth of our group, who were without a doubt, open to the Holy Spirit.

Our Lady must have known how much I missed my own family. The happiness these teens brought into my life was special. Ivana and Mate, brother and sister from my host's guest house in Medjugorje, and whom I love as my own, joined our little group of disciples as we journeyed up the mountain. There was no language barrier between the children. The language of love in their hearts was universal.

With tears they couldn't hold back, Mary Margaret's parents, Jeannie and Gino, thanked everyone for the love they showed their little daughter. Gino discovered during the week that, "If every one of you loved Mary Margaret that much, can you imagine how much more love God must have for all of us!"

It took me a while to realize how much love God has for all of us, for within two weeks of my return from Medjugorje, I nearly failed to answer the call to trust in God's love through any adversity.

Chapter Thirteen

David's Journey

I went around in circles at least a dozen times trying to write this chapter, each time more difficult than the last. This was one chapter that I had never planned on writing. I just didn't know where to begin. The pain of losing a loved one was deep, but the graces that I was blessed with were Our Lady's way of helping me see the light of Christ. Without the gift of faith, those days would have been among my darkest.

"The Lord is close to the brokenhearted." (Ps 34:19) The words of the Responsorial Psalm helped wipe away my tears on a day I needed to be reassured that the Lord was indeed near to my broken heart. If I didn't truly believe those words, there would be no purpose in writing my story. If I didn't believe in the reassuring Love of Jesus and Mary in my life, I could not have gone on with this work. But that would have been just another unconscious effort to avoid further pain.

On the morning of my birthday, April 2, 1987, at Mass I asked Our Blessed Lord for a very special gift. I didn't specify any particular gift....simply open to any gift God wanted to grace me with. Soon after, I received a telephone call that my nephew, David, had died hours before. "Impossible!" I thought at first, "God wouldn't take him away from us just like that!" I wrestled with God's purpose as I was overcome by the sting of David's death. Ultimately, however, my faith brought me to believe that the Divine Architect of the Universe, God Himself, has not built stairways of faith that lead to nowhere. I was amazed to think that, if I had gone to Medjugorje when I wanted to go at the end of March, I would have been away when David died. *"There is an appointed time for everything and a time for every affair under the heavens."* (Eccl 3:1)

The jolt of David's death left me feeling so alone. I subconsciously alienated myself from a God who would take him away from us without any warning. To our children I said, "We really need to place our trust in God, especially at this time." But it was a difficult task for me to live that example. It was easy to love God when everything was going right. I prayed to Our Lady to help me turn to her Son when I found it almost impossible to do so.

God's ever-present love appeared in a note sent to me from Nashville. A Baptist friend opened my heart once again to Our Lord. "Penny, God has prepared you for this in such a special way that you must be thankful for the guidance he has given you in the past, and which He will continue to give you."

My friend was so right. I thought back to my journey to Medjugorje only two weeks before David's death. The gift of that unexpected pilgrimage was surely Jesus allowing Mary to help strengthen my faith through prayer and witnessing. Our Lord helped me remember that David's life did have a purpose. I recalled a chance meeting our group had with Fr. Svet at the bottom of Mount Podbrdo, otherwise known as Apparition Hill. Mary Margaret's parents, Jeanine and Gino, asked Father to pray for their daughter. Father explained that he would pray for happiness. He told the group at the base of the mountain that I knew what he meant by this prayer. It was happiness that Father prayed for three years ago when we brought our David to St. James. Undeniably, his prayers were answered.

Many within the group were in tears after Father prayed for Mary Margaret. They were upset that he didn't pray for her to be healed of cystic fibrosis. I knew, and I experienced what Father meant by praying for happiness. I prayed in the depths of my heart that they would receive the same grace.

The need to understand the depths of God's mystery and how David's life profoundly touched others was no longer important to me. Through a special grace of Our Lady, I knew how my life had been changed through David. I gave glory to God for that change, and I thanked Our Lady for helping me see Christ more clearly through David's eyes.

I miss David with all my heart. For a while, I wrote to Our Lady every day to ask for help and guidance. I also wrote to David and asked Our Lady in prayer to bring this letter to my nephew sealed with my immeasurable love.

"My Sweet David,

My heart aches as I write to you, and I find it almost impossible to suppress the tears. I pray that these tears wash my eyes so that I can see the purpose of God more clearly. Through these tears, I hope the wounds I feel in missing you so are cleansed.

David, so many memories of the past flood my mind. My thoughts are the times I came to see you in the hospital, especially during the past two years. You battled numerous infections that were almost victorious in taking your life. Your mom and dad never left you alone, and I rejoiced when I was called to stay with you in their place. David, I wonder if you remember the Sunday night that my prayer partner, Anthony, came with me to visit you, so that your mom and dad could get some rest. The Holy Spirit filled our evening with conversation without a pause for six hours, and this from a man who finds it almost impossible to open up to others. You touched the lives of so many, just like that night with Anthony and me as you lay there helpless. I realize now, my silent gem, that God's strength was in your weakness. *"My grace is sufficient for you, for power is made perfect in weakness."* (2 Cor 12:9)

I remember in particular a midnight call from your mom. Your seizures that afternoon had left you inordinately lifeless. There was little hope you would make it through the night. I never prayed over the telephone before, and at first it was awkward. Your mom knew the importance of our praying together, but I was still learning. Our Lady's intercession that night allowed the words of the Gospel to be rooted deep within. *"Again, I say to you, if two of you agree on earth about anything for which they are to pray, it shall be granted to them by my heavenly Father. For where two or three are gathered together in my name, there am I in the midst of them."* (Mt 18:19-20). We knew that God was with us, and He answered our prayers and blessed you with the healing needed to survive when the odds were undeniably against you that night. While watching you lie there suffering, I felt I could accept the fact that God was calling you home to Himself...but you pulled through.

But this time it was different. There was no prior hospital stay, and I preferred to ignore the inevitable. I concentrated on a note sent home by your teacher just the week before. It said that you were more alert and even smiling and making noises. Oh, David, were you smiling because you heard our Eternal Father whisper that He would soon take you home? And so, on April 1, 1987, your little heart stopped, and your new life began.

David, I pray with all my heart that I didn't let Our Lord and Our Blessed Mother down, when through my tears, my pain, and my confusion I doubted the message that we received in Medjugorje. I cried and cried in my bewilderment, "What did it mean, Mary gives you hope?" We had asked Jesus to heal you, and now you are gone.

I will never hold you in my arms again. The last time I held you close was at a Mass that we had in honor of Our Blessed Mother, just a month before you went home to God! Most of the eighty people who gathered together that afternoon had been indirectly introduced to Our Lady of Medjugorje through you. It was your dad's faith in taking you on a pilgrimage to Medjugorje, essentially unheard of, that encouraged countless others to fulfill their journey of faith. I sat during the rosary before the Mass with you nestled close to me. I give glory to God for every minute of those last precious hours we had in the chapel that afternoon. I wish I had known that God was going to call you home. Imagine if I had known that day that I'd be kissing you for the last time. The pain would have been unbearable. Oh, David, I marvel how the Lord knows what's best for us. I felt such peace, as if we were in our own little world. Praying with my eyes closed, my mind drifted back to the apparition room in which I believed Our Lady was present and we were specially blessed. I had that same beautiful feeling as I held you that afternoon.

Even now, I find consolation while I close my eyes for a minute and listen to the church bells ringing in the distance. The sound that echoes is *Salve Regina*. This song never fails to fill my heart with such joy as the faithful in St. James sing it each evening at the beginning of Mass. To me, David, these are little signs from Our Mother Mary that I should continue this witness, no matter how many times I say there's no way that I can. I need to allow Our Blessed Lord to work through my grief. Please pray with me that Our Lady fills me with that grace.

I took the news of your death so hard. Someone said that it's not that God took you home, but that I must believe with all my heart that we were giving you back to God. That was extremely hard for me, as it was so difficult for all of us. I'll never forget having to call your godfather at work to tell him the news. I never knew my Mike to cry before. His love for you was probably deeper than mine. David, how much it must have hurt him to keep his love inside.

My being alone that morning was providential. I could not have suppressed the one-sided screaming match I had with Our Lord. I was so hurt and wouldn't allow His unfailing sympathy to penetrate my soul. I cried through the morning, "O God, why? David's work on this earth is not yet finished." Do you believe that? Here I was telling God that His purpose for your life on earth had not been completed.

I avoided praying because I was confused and even disappointed in Our Lady. It's hard for me to admit this,

David, because I love Our Blessed Mother with all my heart. I really felt let down. Over and over, I questioned what it means that "Mary gives you hope"? Finally, I prayed on my knees in front of my statue of Our Lady holding her lifeless Son in her arms, and I soon began to feel I wasn't alone in my sadness.

The grace of beginning to understand Our Lady's message of hope silently filled my heart. After Jesus' death, the disciples had but a small shred of hope that Jesus' prophecy would be fulfilled. But Mary persevered in her firm belief and hope that Jesus would rise in glory. Mary's hope was realized in the glory of Our Lord's resurrection. Your dad and I asked if Jesus would heal you, and the hope that we received in Our Lady's answer was realized through your death.

David, I do believe with all my heart that Heaven is Paradise and everyone there is whole. I imagine you with little Matthew, my first love from my volunteer days at Cerebral Palsy. You are playing hide and seek in that field of daisies, with Jesus and Mary so proud of you both for all you have suffered. Your perfect healing has been granted, for you are without disabilities with Our Lord. Our hope for you is not shattered; it has been fulfilled. Through a special grace in the face of disappointment, my hope has developed and grown stronger. I have a choice: give in to discouragement or hope in God. Our Lady is my guide, and prayer is my strength. **"Today I** am calling you to open yourselves more to God, so that He can work through you. For as much as you open yourselves, you will receive the fruits from it." (March 6, 1986.)

September 11, 1986: "Dear Children! For these days when you celebrate the cross with joy, I wish your cross to be joyful. Dear children, pray that you can accept sickness and suffering with love like Jesus. Only in that way can I give you the graces of healing with the joy that Jesus allows."

David, your dad was asked to share his feelings at your wake. Everyone knew how difficult it was for him as he spoke through gentle tears. He said, "Yes, it was hard taking care of David when he was alive, but it's going to be harder not taking care of him." He continued, "I know I'm being selfish in wanting David to remain with us longer. Now he is at peace, and we know he is among the Communion of Saints. As our suffering was emotional, compared to that of David's physical, I was blessed to realize it had redemptive value. It was a special calling. I thank God for all the sleepless nights that we had with David. I just wish they were back again."

Your dad turned our sadness momentarily to joy when he said, "Now I know that I have to be good, because I want to join David in Heaven someday." Yes, David, the graces of healing with the joy that Jesus allows, exemplify Our Lady's message as your mom and dad share how they celebrated your cross with joy.

Father gave his homily at your funeral Mass, and he spoke about how Our Blessed Lord came into this world as a helpless child, completely dependent on Mary and Joseph. He shared how your own helplessness brought a whole community together. I remember when you first moved to Pennsylvania. You came home from the Institute for the Achievement of Human Potential where they taught your parents an intense therapy program. Your mom and dad learned that, along with a team of volunteers working twelve to fourteen hours a day, your brain could develop to allow you to see, to hear, and to become mobile. They were to undertake this program with a firm commitment that there would be no days off, not even Christmas.

Not knowing where they were going to find these volunteers, your mom and dad sought out the body of Christ, the Church. That Sunday, your pastor spoke about a new family moving into the parish who would need people who weren't afraid to give of themselves. The call was to help in a developmental program for a special child named David. It would be demanding, and he added that the program would need volunteers seven days a week. Your mom said that those who might be interested could sign at the altar. Father said to keep in mind that if anyone wanted to make this commitment, it was to be done for Our Lord, in front of the Blessed Sacrament.

The response was incredible. Over seventy-five people ranging in age from seven to seventy volunteered. The teams consisted of whoever could make it at specific times, and many were of various faiths. We were able to see the certainty of Our Lady's warning that God doesn't separate religions, only man does. With everyone helping you, David, and praying together, one couldn't help but feel the presence of God.

David, not only did you bring a community together in love and prayer, you also brought our family together. It was beautiful to see how much love Mike and our children had within as they celebrated your life as it was. Their love was always there. Like myself in the beginning, accepting your weakness nurtured that love.

One time, we came to visit with my two nephews, Tommy and Joseph. All the adults and the kids gathered around as you lay motionless on your exercising table. We celebrated being together as we banged pots and blew whistles to stimulate your hearing. To someone outside the house, it probably sounded like a circus. Your slightest response filled us with tremendous joy and encouragement. Even the children wouldn't give up. Tommy slipped away to be alone with you and excitedly called me into your room to show me that you had crawled a few centimeters. Oh, David, how you struggled to please us, as we cheered when you picked up your head ever so slightly. You helped us to thank God for the health we all take for granted. You taught us all to love, and Our Lord taught us to give of ourselves through you.

David, do you remember Our Lord's words, *"Blessed are they who mourn, for they will be comforted."* (Mt 5:4)? Well, before I end this letter, I'd like to share with you how Our Lord sent His Holy Spirit, The Comforter, upon us last evening. I was visiting at the nursing home with my friends who have multiple handicaps. About ten minutes before I was ready to leave, I realized I had missed seeing Rosie. Rosie is in her mid-thirties and confined to a wheelchair. Her verbal abilities are a tremendous blessing and allow us to share without any problems. She had already retired for the evening, so I slipped in to kiss her goodnight. She said she had been trying for the longest time to get some sleep but couldn't. You see, David, one of her closest friends joined you last week in Heaven. Rosie was so worried about whether Linda was with God. As she asked me to pray with her, I was blessed to feel her emptiness. My heart broke for the pain she was in, and the tears I tried to conceal were a great opening for Rosie and me to surrender our pain to our Lord together. *"Cast all your worries upon him because he cares for you."* (1 Pt 5:7)

I shared my news about you. "Try to understand, Rosie, that Linda is no longer blind in Heaven. She will never have to be fed through a tube in her stomach, ever again." In the same light, *"Those that sow in tears shall reap rejoicing."* (Ps 126:5) Rosie realized what I meant about the gift of tears. The more we loved, the more we grieve, and we certainly should not try to conceal how much we love.

David, I don't have all the answers. But I do believe what is written: *"We do not want you to be unaware, brothers, about those who have fallen asleep, so that you may not grieve like the rest, who have no hope."* (1 Thes 4:13), I was able to share my belief in your new life last night, and Rosie's face radiated as she was able to see Linda whole. Love does not end with death but only becomes purified. In Medjugorje, Our Lady gave us hope. That hope, David, was not for your father and I alone. It is for all of those who allow Our Blessed Mother to guide them to realize the glory in the Resurrection. It is a hope beyond measure.

David, please pray for me, that, to the end of my life in this school of love, I may learn to return my love to Jesus and Mary, who have given me such wondrous proofs of their love, through you and through Chucky. Thank you for all you taught us in your silent ways and for the happiness you brought into all of our lives.

I Love You and I Miss You,

Until we're together in the arms of Jesus and Mary,

"I Will Not Forget You…"

(Is 49:15)

Aunt Penny"

Chapter Fourteen

The Gift of Faith

"For by grace you have been saved through faith, and this is not from you; it is the gift of God." (Eph. 2:8) The gift of faith that I received was through the intercession of Our Blessed Mother. I learned this from Fr. Ciszek. "We do not merit faith. God gave it to us as a free gift, but it is ours to preserve or to lose. It is ours to cherish or to take for granted."

But I didn't cherish my faith nearly as much as I would a tangible gift from Our Lord. I wished I would win the lottery because there was so much I felt I could do for others with the money. Only now, after all these years, do I finally realize that it's not money Our Lord wants me to share. It's something more valuable and priceless than that. It's His gift of faith.

It was difficult for me at first to understand how essential it is to be aware of my faith. Not only to be aware of it, but also to pray to Our Lady for the grace to help guard it. Father Ciszek taught, "We must make faith the unspoken principle that guides our every action, the center of our being and of all that we do each day. It must become as real for us, as necessary to our lives as the air we breathe – for without it our lives have no meaning, and our souls may die." Father was gentle but steadfast in trying to help me understand that working to strengthen my faith would be an ongoing struggle.

Fr. Ciszek helped me realize the truth in his words: "We are not alone in our faith. We are members of the Church, the Mystical Body, the kingdom of God here on earth. We are members of this Church through Baptism – the sacrament of the life of faith – and it is in and through the Church that Christ has given us the means to strengthen our faith: His sacraments." He also taught: "If we are serious about preserving our faith, we must surely make use of the sacraments – especially the sacrament of the Eucharist and of Penance, our means of peace and of reconciliation with God." I gradually began to treasure these sacraments.

April 3, 1986: **"Dear Children! I wish to call you to a living of the Holy Mass. There are many of you who have sensed the beauty of the Holy Mass, but there are also those who come unwillingly. I have chosen you, dear children, but Jesus gives you His graces in the Mass. Therefore, consciously live the Holy Mass and let your coming to it be a joyful one. Come to it with love and make the Mass your own. Thank you for having responded to my call."**

When I began to pray that one decade of the rosary in 1983, I also became more conscious of the importance of attending Sunday Mass. I'm amazed how Our Lady guides us very gently and in our own time. It wasn't until six months later that I paid attention to the call to receive Our Blessed Lord more frequently in Holy Communion.

A seed was planted simply in one single sentence. Valerie from the Molloy College prayer group asked, "How often do you go to Mass?" When I replied, "Every Sunday," she was atypically quiet. I had no idea what she was hinting at because I thought that Sundays were enough. But that evening, our conversation made me think that I was being told something and was not listening.

The next day was the first Friday of the month, and I remembered from grammar school the devotion to the nine First Fridays. It was the promise of Our Lord to St. Margaret Mary Alacoque in which she was told: "I promise thee in the excessive mercy of My Heart that My all-powerful love will grant to all those who communicate on the First Friday in nine consecutive months the grace of final penitence; they shall not die in my disgrace nor without receiving their Sacraments; My Divine Heart shall be their safe refuge in this last moment."

That promise was the incentive I needed to help wake me up early the next morning. It was the first time in over twenty years that I ever went to a Mass other than on a Sunday, and I still wondered why I was going. At 6:30 a.m. my silent complaint to Our Lady that I could be sleeping ceased the minute the priest announced that it was the feast day of St. Charles.

Immediately, I felt Our Lady might have been telling me that my brother, whose baptized name was Charles, needed more sacrifices. I left church that morning feeling extremely close to my brother once again, and God knew how much I needed that. Offering my Mass for Chucky was the link that gave birth to my plea to Our Lady to help me try to attend Mass every day.

My desire, placed before the throne of God, was granted. I received an increasing love for the Mass. I believed that I knelt amidst a multitude of holy angels who were also present at every Mass, and the infinite value of the Mass entered my heart.

For a whole year, I loved that early morning hour. It was so quiet, and it seemed to be mine alone with Our Lord. The eagerness to wake up in the twinkling of an eye was undeniably a grace from Our Lady. August 25, 1987: **"Dear Children! Seek from God the graces which He is giving you through me. I am ready to intercede with God for all that you seek so your holiness may be complete. Therefore, dear children, do not forget to seek, because God has permitted me to obtain graces for you."** I experienced a fullness in receiving the Eucharist every day like no other. My effort to attend Mass, despite any circumstance, never ceased to amaze me. I never imagined I would be walking in a snowstorm at six in the morning to attend Mass. On my return home that same morning, right in front of my house,

I slipped on a patch of ice. Here I was, flat on my back, looking up to the heavens, saying, "Thanks, Lord, I owe you one!"

My sensitivity to the Eucharist was like day and night. In the past, I'd received Communion without much thought. As Our Lady gently led me to prayer, she now gently led me to a deeper awareness of the Real Presence of Jesus in the Eucharist under the appearance of bread and wine. *"For my flesh is true food, and my blood is true drink. Whoever eats my flesh and drinks my blood remains in me and I in him."* (Jn 6: 55-57) As I uttered, "Lord, I am not worthy that you should enter under my roof but only say the word and my soul shall be healed," I came to realize the greatest healing the Lord extends to us is in the Eucharist.

I was indirectly asked to share the peace that I received from going to daily Mass. My children, Michael and Donna, supposed that if they came to Mass with me, afterward they would just have to walk across the street to our parish school. I didn't want to discourage them, and I was proud that they were with me, but it was something I had to get used to. Instead of walking up to Communion preparing for Christ to dwell within me, my thoughts easily diverted to who was stepping on whose heels!

I prayed to Our Lady for the return of my peace. That prayer was granted through the gift of reading the book by St. Therese of Lisieux, *A Story of a Soul*. The exemplification of her 'Little Ways' were truly inspirational. One portion in her autobiography described how the continuous humming of a sister next to her in chapel constantly distracted her. St. Therese put the sound of the sister's humming to music in her mind. No longer was it a disturbance, but a blessing. This lesson from St. Therese allowed me to enjoy the presence of Michael and Donna and all the music that accompanied them.

Fr. Ciszek also spoke about all being members of the Body of Christ. Once we received a special blessing that actually enabled us to experience that grace. It happened at a time when my son Michael was ill for over a week. At Mass, the priest asked if anyone had special intentions we wanted to pray for. I found it awkward to speak up, but I knew it was important to ask the congregation to pray for Michael. I mentioned it only one morning, but for the remaining days, Father continued to ask for prayers for him. I told Michael that many people were praying and asking for him, and his smile helped me realize how blessed we were to belong to a body who cares when one of its parts is sick. *"Now you are Christ's body, and individually parts of it."* (1 Cor. 12:27)

Our Lady's message from Medjugorje instructing us how to prepare for Mass was not only a teaching, but also a jewel. She said: **"Those Christians who go to church without preparation, without receiving Holy Communion, without giving thanks, it is better that they do not go because their hearts become hard."** She added: **"When you go to church start preparing for Mass as soon as you leave home and never leave the church without thanking God."** I always had the keys for my car in my hand, even before the priest left the altar. A group of Michael's young friends helped motivate me and others to start to put Our Lady's message into practice.

Michael was having a sleepover with a number of boys in his class. But at 3 a.m., I was at my wits end as to how to quiet them down. I was shocked when I suggested a rosary and they agreed. We talked for nearly an hour after our prayers, mostly about what we could do for Our Lady during the month of October. A few of the boys offered to come to a rosary after the 7:30 a.m. Mass. I was amazed how faithful they were to their commitment. In November, when their promise had expired, a good friend continued to pray the rosary with me every day. The simplicity of this daily rosary that began through the children was how a small group of us became one in spirit. We learned to never leave the church without thanking God.

There is a special moment I witnessed in church every day for many years that always captured my heart. An elderly woman would kneel to pray for a few minutes in front of Our Lady's statue, and as she would turn around to leave, she would blow the rest of us a kiss. From the very first day she did this, I felt as if Our Lady was kissing us, saying, "Thank you for your response to my call."

Receiving the Eucharist daily has undeniably made my life more meaningful. Not only does it continually give me a deeper understanding of the holy mystery of Christ's presence, but also the grace to overcome temptation. At the same time, it has created within me a deep desire to avoid sin. I try to live the Church's teachings. To receive the spiritual treasure of the Body and Blood of Jesus, we are called to be in the state of grace. That is, to be free from mortal sin and pleasing to God. Our Lord instituted the Sacrament of Penance, which allows us to enter the state of grace, when he breathed on his Apostles and gave them power to forgive sins. *"Whose sins you forgive are forgiven then, and whose sins you retain are retained."* (Jn 20:23)

"If Christians went to confession every month, reconciling themselves with God and their neighbors, whole Christian communities would soon be spiritually healed." Church law requires confession of sins once a year. (Code of Canon Law, canon 989) Our Lady's message made me realize the value of the Sacrament of Penance, not only for removing sin, but also as a positive means of spiritual progress. Going to monthly confession helps me look more honestly at my everyday actions and attitudes. I am conscious of my own weaknesses and realize through frequent confession that, if I love God as much as I say I do, I will try harder not to offend Him by my sins, no matter how big or small.

I learned that sins are divided into two classes – mortal sins and venial sins. A venial sin is an offense that does not kill the soul yet displeases God and often leads to mortal sin. St. Teresa of Avila's teaching to confess all sins gives me constant food for thought. She says, "Never fail to confess what we think is a sin even though venial. Pay attention to the venial and fear them as the mortals." I pray to Our Lady to increase my fear of sin. At one time, as God allowed me to continually fall into the same serious sin that I could not free myself of, I came to discover that it was only through weekly confession and the special grace that I received through this humbling experience that I was freed from this personal fault. *"For human beings this is impossible, but for God all things are possible." (Mt 19:26)*

Bishop Sheen once wrote: "There are two ways of knowing how good God is. One is never to lose Him. The other is to lose Him and find Him again." That helps me to describe how the Sacrament of Reconciliation has changed my life. While growing up, I experienced a great feeling coming out of confession. Not only did I believe that my sins were absolved, but many times I felt drawn to confession when I was confused and needed someone to steer me on the right path. I truly felt that God's love, mercy, and patience with me was without measure. However, as the years went on, I lost that child-like faith which I envisioned as the porthole of His love. Undeniably, it was through the Sacraments and Our Lady's repeated cry to *pray, pray, pray*, that I once again discovered how good God is.

St. Augustine once said, "I know what I am, but I'm not what I ought to be." A stronger Christian is what I feel I ought to be. Yet, I realize that only through prayer can I seek to attain that. I continually pray for the grace to open my heart to Mary to allow her to teach me. September 25, 1987: **"Dear Children! Today also I want to call you all to prayer. Let prayer be your life. Dear children, dedicate your time only to Jesus and He will give you everything that you are seeking. He will reveal Himself to you in fullness. Dear children, Satan is strong and is waiting to test each one of you. Pray, and that way he will neither be able to injure you nor block you on the way of holiness. Dear children, through prayer grow all the more toward God from day to day. Thank you for having responded to my call."**

Our Lady's sole desire of bringing us closer and closer to God speaks loud and clear to me through over eighty of her messages on prayer. **"Dear children! Today again I invite you to prayer. You, dear children, do not realize the preciousness of prayer. Now is the time of prayer. Now, nothing else is important. Now, nobody is important except God. Dear children, dedicate yourselves to prayer with special love. Only in that way can God give you graces."**

I never imagined that I would be able to consecrate myself to prayer. But through a deep love, placed in my heart for prayer, I found myself saying with the Psalmist: *"Teach me to do your will, for you are my God."* (Ps 143:10) I experienced a vast number of growing pains believing that no prayer goes unanswered. In February 1985, my husband Mike and I heard the news that a very close friend of ours named John was diagnosed with bone cancer. I was preparing to go to Medjugorje and so the thought came to me to petition Our Lord, through the intercession of Mary, for a healing for John. John's wife, Grace, gave me one of his shirts, and, through a very special grace, it was placed in the apparition room.

John's disease progressed rapidly. When Mike and I visited him two weeks later with the shirt, I found it difficult to come to terms with the fact that he was now paralyzed and confined to a hospital bed. To believe that he would never walk again seemed unreal. I prayed all the more for his healing. To pray for a deeper understanding of the mystery of suffering would lead me to The Cross, and, at this point in time, uniting John's suffering with Christ's was inconceivable to me. I needed to learn so much more about prayer. It never entered my mind to pray for God's strength during this crucial time, or to even trust in Him more, I just didn't. My prayers were on one track only.

I hung onto every ray of hope believing that John would be healed. Even when we visited him in Sloan Kettering Cancer Center, I still trusted that God wouldn't let us down.

Grace called me early in the morning of May 1 to tell me that John had died during the night, and I was brokenhearted. I cried myself back to sleep saying, "Why, God? Why couldn't John be healed?" I don't know how long I slept or what transpired during this time, but I know that, upon waking, my sadness was gone. Looking back, I'm convinced it was Our Lady's blanket of maternal love, sympathy, and enlightenment that covered me while I slept. Upon calling Grace, a true spirit of joy prompted me to say, "Grace, we prayed to the Blessed Mother for her intercession for John, and guess what? Our prayers were answered!" I trusted implicitly that it was through the grace of Mary's intercession that John was ready to meet Our Lord. Considering that he was taken home on the first day of May, the month dedicated to Mary, I felt confident of Our Lady's assistance at the hour of his death. *"Whatever you ask for in prayer with faith, you will receive."* (Mt 21:22)

I have learned that only through prayer are the words *patience* and *perseverance* viable in my life. We live in a society of instant gratification. Thoughts of prayers being instantly answered are common. But I began each day reading the lives of the Saints. Through them, I learned about perseverance in prayer. They are to be our role models. We are all called to be Saints. My faith in God is minuscule compared to theirs, yet I am haunted to follow their example.

And with patience, for more than three years I prayed that Mike and our children would come to Medjugorje with me. The family that I lived with would ask, "Penny, next time you come back with your family?" If they only knew how much that meant to me. My kids would laugh when I asked them to join me, yet I received a special grace to persevere in prayer and not give up hope. St. Monica prayed for her son, St. Augustine, for seventeen years. That was a definite affirmation to believe in the impossible. Our Lady must have pulled some strings in Heaven because the children and I did share Medjugorje for a week during the summer of 1987. It was a dream come true. *"Therefore I tell you, all that you ask for in prayer, believe that you will receive it and it shall be yours."* (Mark 11:24)

Chapter 15

Second Half of Life

"The Lord became my protector. He brought me out to a place of freedom; he saved me because he delighted in me." This was the Entrance Antiphon at Mass this morning on March 5, 2019, which for me marked the 35th Anniversary of when I first traveled to Medjugorje with my nephew David and his father John.

Thirty five years still seems unimaginable to me, especially as we arrived home only last week (writing in the fall of 2019) from my 102nd pilgrimage to Medjugorje. To say that Our Lord saved me because he delighted in me is a reality that every day I still try to process because of my unworthiness. Through the grace of God, Our Lady has brought me to cherish my faith through these 35 years, and I am ever grateful. Back in 1981, the year before Chucky took his life, I did not even attend Mass on Christmas. I was too busy getting ready to host Mike's family in our home for dinner. Before I was blessed to be broken by Chucky's suicide, I am embarrassed to say I felt the unflattering term of being a Chreaster (Catholics who only attend Mass on Christmas and Easter) possibly applied to me. I say blessed because through Chucky's suicide I found a path through Christ as to how to deal with the heartbreak.

It has been an incredible journey; a journey of love, pain, prayer, obstacles, healing, struggles, and an abundance of joy, grace, and a daily conversion I strive for but so often fail to do. Our Lady's message of September 25, 2016 really speaks to my heart and describes my walk with God alongside of Our Lady of Medjugorje as my teacher: "**Dear Children! Today, I am calling you to prayer. May prayer be life to you. Only in this way will your heart be filled with peace and joy. God will be near you and you will feel Him in your heart as a friend. You will speak with Him as with someone whom you know and, little children, you will have a need to witness, because Jesus will be in your heart and you, united in Him. I am with you and love all of you with my motherly love. Thank you for having responded to my call.**"

Yes, I have a "need to witness" and also a responsibility. "*Much will be required of the person entrusted with much, and still more will be demanded of the person entrusted with more.*" (Lk 12:48) I received grace upon grace, but also struggle upon struggle. It is through daily Mass and beginning a formative life of prayer that I am able to continue my journey. Every time I fall, Our Lady picks me up and brushes me off and places me gently back on my feet to begin again; a constant job for her. The most important lesson I have learned is to keep my eyes fixed on God's goodness rather than my own wretchedness.

February 2, 2017: "**Dear Children! You are striving to offer every day of your life to my Son, you are trying to live with Him, you who are praying, sacrificing – you are hope in this peaceless world. You are rays of light of my Son, a living gospel, you are my beloved apostles of love. My son is with you. He is with those who think of Him – those who pray. But in the same way, He is patiently waiting for those who do not know Him. Therefore, you, apostles of my love, pray with the heart and with your works show the love of my Son. This is the only hope for you, and this is also the only way to eternal life. I, as a mother, I am here with you. Your prayers directed to me are the most beautiful roses of love for me. I cannot but be where I sense the scent of roses. There is hope. Thank you.**"

In the fall of 1986, several friends who had traveled to Medjugorje were invited to a mutual friend's house for prayer and fellowship. Sister Mary Frances brought a priest along who was very moved by our little group. Father suggested, "Take what you have and center it on The Eucharist!" He suggested forming a prayer group and identified some key positions necessary to lead the group. Fino, as president, immediately took his responsibility very seriously with a long-term vision. He suggested we call his lawyer on Monday to form a non-profit corporation. Our mission to help spread Our Lady's messages was incorporated as a non-profit organization named, "Our Lady Queen of Peace Prayer Group." Sister Mary Frances invited our newly formed prayer group to her convent to celebrate a Mass for Peace on the second Sunday of every month. Changing locations a few times, this Mass for Peace continued every second Sunday for 24 years until 2010.

Our prayer group began publishing a one-page flyer with Our Lady's monthly message and invited people to our Mass for Peace. This soon turned into a four-page newsletter entitled "Mary's Mantle." Despite having no experience in publishing, I had the responsibility of this work. I met weekly with Sal, a fellow pilgrim, in an empty classroom at Fordham University where he taught me how to layout a newsletter. I was driving home from Fordham in the Bronx that night to my home in Long Island after 10 p.m. I needed to be at a friend's print shop the next day with my material. That is when I started to believe in miracles and guardian angels. Somehow, despite my working full time, caring for 3 children ages 10, 12, and 14, and my husband working evening hours, "Mary's Mantle" became a reality.

Fr. Slavko Barbaric (1946-2000), who is credited with creating the prayer program in Medjugorje, often said that prayer groups would change the world. With more pilgrims returning home to the New York area from Medjugorje in 1987, a new prayer group of 20 people began meeting on the last Monday of every month for prayer, adoration, and fellowship. Our time together created a bond and new friendships from the New York, New Jersey, and Connecticut areas. We met for the next 19 years, until 2006.

Once this small group was incorporated in 1987, we began to organize our first formal pilgrimage and planned three or four trips to Medjugorje annually. It was all a learning curve and different board members would lead these groups. We continued to stay with the family I met in Medjugorje in 1985, Jozo and Marica Tunin Vaslij and I could say we all "grew up" together. After my children's first visit in the summer of 1987, I continued to bring them during the next few summers with our pilgrim groups. Today, my children and Tunin Vaslij's children are like family. We have attended each other's weddings, children's baptisms, and First Holy Communions. So many of the pilgrims who have traveled with us have bonded with the amazing Tunin Vaslij family, and when pilgrims return a second or third time, they feel like they are back home.

On a flight home from Medjugorje in February 1987, a fellow pilgrim named Grace requested a favor. I very much admired Grace. She was a very holy woman, and her mission was to pray for priests. She asked me to join her in this mission. Her invitation took hold of my heart. "**In a special way, my motherly heart loves the shepherds. Pray for their blessed hands. Thank you.**"

If I shouted Our Lady's message from the rooftops, it would have very little impact, compared to a priest witnessing his love for Our Lady. It is often said that if a mother and father pray, then the family prays. Yet when a priest prays, the entire parish prays. If a priest holds Our Lady in his heart and experiences Medjugorje, what a formidable influence he can be.

I prayed to find a priest who would work with our parish. In October, 1988, a parishioner named Kathy directed me to a new priest who had been to Medjugorje. What a beautiful and powerful answer to my prayers! I could write an entire book on the gift of working with Fr. James Moyna, OP, for the next eighteen years.

Fr. Moyna and I started a rosary group for children in our parish school every Monday and celebrated New Year's Eve with Midnight Mass and fellowship for years. We had permission from our pastor to expose the Blessed Sacrament every Friday after morning Mass until 5 p.m. We hosted Sunday night rosary with contemplative meditations that lasted an hour each week. We invited groups of parishioners to consecrate themselves to Our Blessed Mother, through the 33-day spiritual exercise based on the writings of St. Louis de Montfort. We initiated all-night vigils for different intentions, and Fr. Moyna led us on countless pilgrimages. Within four months of his meeting me, Father stepped aside because this work for Our Lady was becoming so very demanding. I left at his rectory a cassette tape for Father of a visionary from the Ukraine, Josyp Terelya, with a song entitled, "Feed my Lambs, Feed my Sheep." A few days later, Fr. Moyna called and said, "Whatever I can do for you, day or night, I'm here for you." I knew that this response was to Our Lady, and I was grateful that he united with me in responding to Our Lady's call.

Throughout the years, Fr. Moyna and I volunteered one night a week at a cancer care unit and another with our extra-ordinary friends with cerebral palsy. We often brought friends from our Sunday night rosary group to visit the residents at their home. To give our new friends who had CP a real sense of purpose, we suggested staging a Christmas pageant. Two days before the show, we thought we would never be able to pull this off, yet our prayer partners from our Sunday night rosary group rallied to help us, bringing stage lights and creating costumes for each one in the play. The play truly touched the hearts of the staff, and our special needs friends were in their glory. It was a beautiful friend-ship; and when we celebrated Fr. Moyna's 25th Anniversary of Ordination, the entire dance floor was filled with our friends in wheelchairs.

It wasn't our prayer group that drew Fr. Moyna back to us. Our Lady gave him the grace to say yes, and Father's love and commitment to his priesthood began to flourish. While Father came from a very small family, God's love within him touched so many souls, both young and old, and before too long his spiritual family was larger than life. Thirty-three priests concelebrated his funeral Mass on December 5, 2005, with over 900 people in the congregation. It was an inspiring testimony to Fr. Moyna's commitment to our prayer group and the *fruit of his fiat*, his *yes*.

Fr. Moyna became like a sixth member of my family. After ten years living in our parish, my husband invited Fr. Moyna to live with us. He spent the last five years of his life living at our home and continued to preach and celebrate Mass at a local parish. He worked with me on many of Our Lady's projects, including "Mary's Mantle," which grew to eight pages and a readership of over 6,000 people. Many nights our little newsletter would be spread out on my dining room table where Fr. Moyna and I argued about microscopic editing matters. Father was an intellect, a civil engineer, and a talented artist. He would design the cover, right up until the last minute, as we were leaving for the printer. His artwork was acclaimed by many. How blessed I was to work so closely with him!

In the spring of 1989, Fr. Moyna and I met a young man in a wheelchair at a local preserve with his two-year-old son, Conor. Detective Steven McDonald was a third-generation New York City police officer, and we became immediate friends. On July 12, 1986, while on duty in Central Park, Steven was shot three times in the head, neck, and stomach by a 15-year-old boy. Steven was 29 years old at the time of the shooting and had been married just eight months to Patti Ann, who was 23 years old and three months pregnant with Conor. Steven survived the shooting and remained paralyzed from the neck down for the remaining 30 years of his life.

In the aftermath of the shooting, the McDonald family became close friends with John Cardinal O'Connor, the Archbishop of New York. On March 1, 1987, Cardinal O'Connor baptized Conor in St. Patrick's Cathedral. On the day of his son's baptism and before Steven regained his physical ability to speak, Patti Ann spoke for them and shared that they forgave Steven's assailant. For 30 years Steven shared his story of forgiveness, traveling endlessly to talk with school children, politicians, countless parishes, law enforcement officials, educators, and people of all ages, faiths, and walks of life.

My journey and Steven's were interwoven from the time we met. We lived in the next town from each other, and Patti Ann's chaplain from high school, Fr. Farley, was one of my closest friends. On one of my first trips to Medjugorje in 1986, I traveled with Fr. Farley. When we met Fr. Moyna two years later, the three of us were united in helping to spread Our Lady's messages from Medjugorje.

In January 1991, I asked Fr. Farley if we could have an all-night vigil on the First Friday of each month to pray to end abortion and for an increase in respect for all human life. Fr. Farley agreed to host the all-night vigil in his parish. In May, Fr. Farley celebrated our first Mass at 9 p.m. and continued alternating with Fr. Moyna between the evening and the morning Mass at 5 a.m. Our First Friday Vigil for

Life continues to this day from 7 to 11 p.m., and Steven would attend as often as he was able throughout the years.

In 1995, Steven suggested that we get together at his home on the second Thursday of each month to pray for priests. This prayer group for priests continued for twenty years until our chaplain was called home by God. We continue our prayers for priests by uniting for a weekly Holy Hour every Thursday that continues to this day.

In June 1991, war broke out in Croatia, the War of Independence which lasted from 1991 to 1995, so we withdrew from going to Medjugorje until 1993. In 1992, our group began traveling to different Marian Shines in Europe and Canada and included the Holy Land as one of our yearly destinations.

A group of my new spiritual friends who had introduced me to Fr. Walter Ciszek were very involved in reported apparitions of St. Michael and Our Lady in Northern Spain. Nestled in the snow-capped Pena Sagra Mountain range is a little town of San Sebastian de Garabandal. One of the four young visionaries, named Conchita, was a close friend of two of my friends. Through them, I met Conchita in 1984.

The happenings in Garabandal began in 1961 and continued for four years. Some events were quite extraordinary, and Our Lady was reported to be giving messages that seemed to be closely connected to those in Fatima and Medjugorje. Our Lady's urgent call to pray for the priesthood over fifty years ago in Garabandal was one of the focal points of the messages. Almost monthly, in Medjugorje, Our Lady concludes her message to Mirjana Soldo on the second of each month with a plea to pray for her shepherds. I was inspired to include Garabandal in the same yearly pilgrimage to Fatima, Compostela, and Lourdes as the link between Garabandal and Medjugorje couldn't be clearer to me.

In the spring of 2006, Fr. Jozo Zovko, was invited to visit New York. He had been pastor of St. James parish in Medjugorje when the apparitions began in 1981 and was imprisoned for his faith. I had known Fr. Jozo since the early 90's when I was blessed to be among a group of twelve people on a four-day retreat with him at his parish in Tihaljina. Fr. Jozo's English-speaking translator was a friend of ours from Medjugorje, and in 2006 Fr. Jozo was looking for parishes in the US where he might speak. A member of our prayer group asked his pastor in Point Lookout, Long Island, to host the event. The pastor had been to Medjugorje and immediately welcomed Fr. Jozo. A lot of planning was needed, so the pastor asked our prayer group to join with their parish council to help plan the event. We did not know if 100 or 1,000 people would attend a Mass with Fr. Jozo, and we were delighted when over 1,200 people joined in a three-hour prayer program on November 7, 2006. That evening there was a crowd waiting in line to enter the parish center where Mass was being celebrated. I did not know how to keep all those who were waiting in line from being restless. I was given a bullhorn and began my first public recitation of the rosary to bring peace to the crowd and to welcome the Holy Spirit. It was an amazing evening, and many of us felt Our Lady's rays of grace pouring upon us.

The pastor of Our Lady of the Miraculous Medal Parish became one of my cherished friends and asked if we would come to his weekly parish prayer group. This parish prayer group had been praying for several years with less than five to seven members. It was held every Tuesday evening in the rectory basement, and a few people from our prayer group united with theirs. They welcomed us with open arms. Together we prayed to the Holy Spirit, who led us as we studied the Scriptures, contemplated the readings for the following Sunday, and then shared the insights we received. The joy and solidarity that filled the rectory basement as we kept one another's intentions deep within our hearts helped us become like family. Mary's words of September 25, 2000, were: **"Renew prayer in your families and form prayer groups. In this way you will experience joy in prayer and togetherness. All those who pray and are members of prayer groups are open to God's will in their hearts and joyfully witness God's love. I wish for a prayer group...I will guide this group and later, when I say so, other groups can be formed in the world."** Our Lady continued, **"I want a prayer group here. I will lead the group and give rules of sanctification to it. Through these rules all others in the world can consecrate themselves."**

In witnessing to Our Lady's interior messages, Jelena Vasilj, who began experiencing Our Lady interiorly with her heart in December, 1982, cooperated with Our Lady in forming a prayer group of about 20 people to make a commitment for four years. As a prayer group leader in Medjugorje, Jelena shared that Our Blessed Mother had provided us with a living model of what a prayer group should be. She provided Jelena with guidance for prayer groups to follow. Members of the prayer group were to remove all fear from their hearts forever and renounce any inordinate desires. They were to avoid television, particularly evil programs, excessive sports that would take away from their prayer life, and the unreasonable enjoyment of food and drink, alcohol, tobacco, and other habits. She urged the prayer group to eliminate all anguish and told them that whoever abandons themselves to God, without any restrictions, does not have room in their heart for anguish.

Our Lady asked that members of the prayer group fast twice a week on bread and water because it is the best fast. Fasting once or twice a week is a form of oneness with the Lord. Our Lady says fasting can stop wars and suspend natural laws. The visionary, Marija Lunetti, stated that there were other forms of fasting, too. People with addictions were to fast from those addictions one day a week. Fasting can be giving up something you enjoy such as television.

Our Lady told Jelena that the group should devote three hours a day to prayer, with a half an hour in the morning and a half an hour in the evening. Included in this time of prayer are Holy Mass and the rosary. She encourages us to set aside moments during the course of the day to pray. These teachings were a foundation to integrate into our prayer groups in New York and on Long Island.

Since 2006, encouraged by the pastor, I made Our Lady of the Miraculous Medal my adopted parish. I asked Father if we could have a Eucharistic Procession to celebrate the feast of Our Lady's Assumption on August 15, 2007, along the main street of this one-square mile beach town. August 15 is known as the Blessing of the Waters day in the Catholic faith. It is the day when the oceans are believed blessed. I didn't have a clue how to do this, yet we had the support of some local parishioners, and I asked for two communities of religious sisters to join us. The August 15 Eucharistic Procession was incredible. Over 150 people joined it. People came out of the local restaurants to see what was going on. Some blessed themselves as we passed. Our flyer welcomed bicycles, strollers, golf carts, and dogs, and we requested that people wear white. After three hours of prayer, a group of us went three blocks away to the ocean to dip our feet into the water. We shared abundant elation and shouted prayers of thanksgiving to the Heavens for such a blessed event. A magnificent feeling of God's love poured down on us. I suspected that evening was a similar encounter for Peter, James, and John on Mount Tabor after the Transfiguration; they just didn't want to leave.

On August 15, 2019, we hosted our 12th Eucharistic Procession with the parish of Our Lady of the Miraculous Medal. It is amazing how for the first nine years, my most challenging struggle was to recruit eight strong men (four men to carry the canopy to protect the Blessed Sacrament and four men to carry Our Lady's statue on a platform) on their shoulders. They also needed to have strength and humility to wear long white albs while doing so. Through the grace of God, I met a man in church who owned a gym. He has a huge following of young men, whom he and a parish priest guide spiritually, so he promised that he would commission the eight men for me. When Anthony arrived two minutes before the 6 p.m. start with his army of eight tattooed men, I was beside myself. God may have taken me to the edge at the last moment, but He always provides!

I recently read that August 15 is one of the five calendar days throughout the year when most souls go to Heaven from Purgatory. Moving forward, I plan to make that announcement and focus on releasing many more souls from Purgatory and adding the Chaplet of Divine Mercy to our prayers during Adoration before Mass.

In November, 2009, the funds for Our Lady Queen of Peace Prayer Group account were absolutely depleted. As the "chief financial officer" of our nonprofit group, I knew in my heart we could not continue to publish our yearly newsletter. Our generous benefactors were now retired and had to take a step back financially, yet I did not want to stop trying to spread Our Lady's messages. I then thought about making a documentary on Medjugorje as a more effective way to reach masses of people. I asked Mate, the son of Jozo and Marica from Medjugorje, to collaborate with me on the film. I knew nothing about producing a film, nor did Mate, but I believe in scripture. *"Ask and it shall be given to you; seek, and you will find; knock and the door will be opened to you."* (Mt. 7:7) I also did not have the money to produce a documentary film. Yet, I made an agreement with my husband, Mike, who respects my mission but never had a desire to go to Medjugorje, that if he would finance the project for me, I would give him my social security checks and pay him back for however long it would take. I estimated it would take 12-13 years to return his loan. To date, I am more than halfway through on my payments. I am grateful for my husband's support and feel it is an honor to take on this work for Our Lady, which is titled "God Exists...The Queen of Peace Speaks from Medjugorje."

It was initially estimated that we could produce this film for a particular amount. It turned out to be almost four times as much to complete the project than originally budgeted. It took almost four years and a second production crew, but our first 1,000 copies of the film were delivered to our door on June 24, 2013, Our Lady's Anniversary of her first appearance in Medjugorje. There were times in the early stages of our work that I would be in confession more often than not, trying to come to peace about where I wanted this work to go and where it was actually going. The priest suggested I spend time in front of the Blessed Sacrament and give my distresses to Our Lord. This advice became a tremendous gift in my life. Our Lady's message on September 25, 1995: **"Dear Children! Today I invite you to fall in love with the Most Holy Sacrament of the Altar. Adore Him, little children, in your parishes and in this way you will be united with the entire world. Jesus will become your friend and you will not talk of Him like someone whom you barely know. Unity with Him will be a joy for you and you will become witnesses to the love of Jesus that He has for every creature. Little children, when you adore Jesus you are also close to me. Thank you for having responded to my call."**

Dedicating one hour a day in Adoration and bringing my production glitches to Jesus and Mary soon became an integral part of my day. My tribulations were unraveled one by one. Father had guided me on the path I needed to complete this work. My desire for time in Adoration brought the words of St. Ignatius to a reality for me. "To withdraw from creatures and repose with Jesus in the Tabernacle is my delight; there I can hide myself and seek rest." I learned to rest in the love of Jesus and trust implicitly in His gift of Divine Providence not only for my work, our film, and my family, but in every aspect of my life. I learned how to bring Him every concern of mine no matter how trivial it may have seemed. Many times, I would come home to Mike and tell him how I had slept for more than half my Holy Hour. Yet, as I rested in the heart of Jesus, His rays of love filled my heart with confidence and love from His Sacred Heart!

Images of My Lifelong Journey

Chucky in his police car and Penny, ages 3 and 5.

(L to R) Clark family photo, Penny, Judi, Mom, Bobby; sitting,
Chucky, Dad & Susan.

Chucky's family in 1982, Stephen, Brian, Chucky & Helen.

(L to R) Sr. Janja, a local parishioner from Medjugorje, and
Penny holding David. March 1984.

Visionary Vicka holding David, Jakov, & Marija. March 1984.

Apparition Hill-Podbrdo.

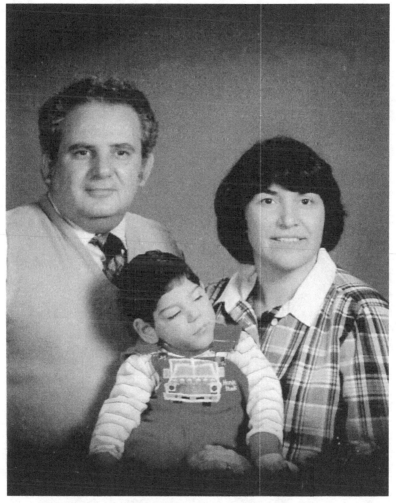

David and his parents, John and Karen.

Penny and David at a family picnic
September 1986

(L to R) Visionaries Jakov and Ivan

Visionary Ivanka, (2nd to left), with Penny & friends
February 1989

Penny with Vicka
Summer 1989

Penny and visionary Marija, 1988.

(L to R) Our host family, Mate, Marica, visionary Mirjana, &
Katarina, as we prepared for our documentary, "God Exists…
The Queen of Peace Speaks from Medjugorje."

Penny with Servant of God, Fr. Walter J. Ciszek, S.J., my first
spiritual director, September 1984.

Penny and Fr. Jozo Zovko, OFM. February, 1990. Fr. Jozo was
imprisoned for his belief in the reported apparitions.

Penny with Dr. Fr. Tomislav Pervan, OFM, the pastor of St.
James in Medjugorje from 1982-1988.

Fr. James Moyna, OP, with Fr. Svetozar Kraljevic, OFM
Summer 2004.

Head of our guesthouse, Jozo, with former and current pastors of
St. James, Fr. Pervan and Fr. Marinko, February 2018.

Our Monthly Cenacle for Priests originated in the home of
Steven and Patti Ann McDonald. Bishop Francisco Garmendia
was our main celebrant in 1995.

Our Tuesday night young adults prayer group, which met at our
house from 1986-1988.

Penny's daughter Donna, age 12, and son Michael, age 14, were
among the Queen of Peace youth group pilgrims in 1989.

Volunteering with special needs friend, Gladys, and sister,
Bernadine, to her left.

Cross Mountain-Mount Krizevac.

Bill O'Reilly, from Inside Edition, interviewing Fr. Philip Pavich, OFM, while he and his crew traveled with Our Lady Queen of Peace Prayer Group to Medjugorje, Summer 1990.

Our Lady Queen of Peace Prayer Group pilgrims in front of the Church of St. James, February 2018.

Penny with Peter Powell, Cinematographer and Producer of
"God Exists," June 2013.

Our guest from Croatia was Fr. Zlatko Sudac. Fr. Sudac received
the first mark of the stigmata, in the form of a cross "imprinted"
on his forehead in 1999. Fr. Zlatko visited with Steven and Patti
Ann McDonald in their home in New York, 2002.

Penny's Angels on Earth, Sr. Mildred Meaney and Sr. Michaelita Fleming, along with Steven McDonald and Penny, October 2006.

(L to R) Natasha Tosic, Liz Shea, with President of 206 Tours, Milanka Lachman, and Linda Antonelli, who were incredibly instrumental in making Steven McDonald's three pilgrimages to Medjugorje possible.

My most treasured gift from God, who I love with all of my
heart   my family, August 2020.

My Final Tribute to Steven McDonald

My friendship with Steven McDonald developed into an extraordinary unity of inspiring one another to a deeper level of prayer and desire to live Our Lady's messages. Every time I traveled to Medjugorje, I envisioned Steven joining us. I was aware of his deep longing to do so. From the smallest detail to the biggest stumbling block, I strategized how we could make it work for him. Each time I would fly to Medjugorje, especially when transferring planes to a smaller local aircraft, I couldn't conceive how Steven could get onto the smaller plane. The staircase was so very narrow that I even envisioned they'd need a cherry picker to bring him to the door. I couldn't imagine the amount of supplies Steven would need to be away for eight days and the cost of the excess baggage, not to mention the cost of the entire pilgrimage. Steven's very life depended on his ventilator. I thought back to my early days in Medjugorje when the electricity or running water would go out for an entire day if there was a severe storm. I would often picture different challenges like how to get Steven into our guest home without a ramp or his need for a full-size bed to accommodate him. In all the years I had been to Medjugorje, I had only seen twin size beds. How would our host family ever get a full-size bed past the doorframe?

Steven was still a member of the police department, although he was in a wheelchair and lived on a respirator. The NYPD retained Steven as an "active member" of the force, and he continued an active career with the NYPD. He was promoted to a first-grade detective just before Christmas 2003, seventeen years after he was shot. To transport him, Steven was assigned an officer who had to be available 24 hours a day, seven days a week. Taking Steven to Medjugorje would mean that he needed to bring two police officers, at least one of his nurses, and several volunteers to provide around the clock nursing care in Medjugorje. Steven would also need a van with a hydraulic lift. There are too many details to mention, and not least among them were the funds needed to accomplish this. It could only have happened by the grace of God and the generosity of many supporters, most importantly his medical staff, to make Steven's first pilgrimage to Medjugorje a reality.

We traveled to Medjugorje with Steven and Patti Ann McDonald for Our Lady's 25th Anniversary of her apparitions, June 25, 2006. We traveled again for the Youth Festival with Steven's son Conor and Patti Ann in 2008 and for a third time in 2011 with his mother Anita and brother Thomas. I can witness to Our Lord's promise *"Therefore I tell you, all that you ask for in prayer, believe that you will receive it and it shall be yours."* (Mk 11:24)

Sharing three pilgrimages with Steven was a desire of a lifetime in my heart, as well as for many of our pilgrims traveling with him. Admittedly, we hoped and prayed for his healing through Our Lady's intercession. On the First Friday of January, 2017, we were stunned with the news that Steven was unconscious and on life support. Following our Vigil for Life, we were invited to Steven's hospital room to pray and possibly say our goodbyes. Everyone in his room prayed with infinite hope that God could work His miracle now, so that the whole world would know that He Exists. Our perfect scenario was that Steven would wake up, be totally healed, and continue to touch souls throughout the world and witness to God's Love and Unfathomable Divine Mercy. On January 10, the same date that my brother Chucky's body was found 34 years prior, Steven entered Eternity. Several people visualized Steven dancing with Our Lady whom he loved with all his heart.

Steven cooperated with the grace to suffer well, and he had the conviction that his suffering was redemptive for countless souls throughout the world. Steven and I once took a road trip to Scranton, PA, to visit a very famous priest who many said had the gift of reading into the heart and souls of men. Like St. John Vianney and St. Pio of Pietrelcina, this senior priest from Scranton, who has been a priest for 65 years and an exorcist in the Diocese of Scranton, PA, for over forty years, was also said to have the gift of reading into the heart and soul of certain individuals. Father asked Steven's driver, nurse, and me to join him and Steven in conversation. Father thanked Steven several times for visiting because

Father was truly and absolutely convinced he was looking at the face of Christ. This priest wasn't the only one to see the sanctity of my friend. At Steven's wake, our Bishop was interviewed and said he wouldn't be surprised if Steven would one day be declared a Servant of God, on his way to being canonized a Saint.

Steven's life of prayer can be summarized in the words of Tertullian, a prolific early Christian author. "Prayer gives the armor of patience to those who suffer, who feel pain, who are distressed. It strengthens the power of grace so that faith may know what it is gaining from the Lord, and understand what it is suffering for the name of God."

Steven's straightforwardness, humility, and love for prayer, especially his devotion to Our Lady Queen of Peace, made countless souls aware of God's enormous love for them. What a treasure it was for me to call him one of my closest friends. I made a promise to Steven that I would write my last chapter if he was healed. Steven has received the ultimate healing. He has met The Lord!

Promise kept. My story is complete.

Words of Encouragement from Conchita Gonzales of Garabandal in Troubling Times
Message of March 19, 2020

"God is detaching us from the securities of this world. In the silence of the Church or in our house, we are now able to make an examination of conscience so we can clean what prevents us from hearing the Voice of God clearly. With sincerity we can ask God to tell us what He wants of us today, and continue to do that every day. And spend as much time as possible with God at church or somewhere in your home or where you find the silence. He is all we need."

From Our Lady Queen of Peace in Medjugorje
Message of September 25, 2021

"Dear children, pray, witness and rejoice with me because the Most High continues to send me to lead you on the way of holiness. Be aware, little children, that life is short, and eternity is waiting for you to give glory to God with your being, with all the saints. Little children, do not worry about earthly things, but long for Heaven. Heaven will be your goal and joy will begin to reign in your heart. I am with you and bless all of you with my motherly blessing. Thank you for having responded to my call."

(L to R) Penny Abbruzzese and Conchita Gonzales

About the Author

Penny Abbruzzese has a strong devotion to Our Blessed Mother and is a religious pilgrims' coordinator, who made her first pilgrimage to Medjugorje in Bosnia-Herzegovina in March, 1984. Since then, Penny has been to Medjugorje more than 100 times with groups from near and far. In the 37 years since her first pilgrimage, Penny has led tours to holy places such as Fatima, Lourdes, Garabandal, and Santiago de Compostela. She has visited shrines in France, Italy, Bavaria, Mexico, Turkey, Greece, Poland, Prague, Vienna, and Israel's Christian holy places.

Working alongside the New York City Croatian Church, which is a sister parish to St. James in Medjugorje, Penny sponsored several visionaries and well-known priests from Medjugorje to speak in New York. As one of the founding officers of a non-profit organization, Our Lady Queen of Peace Prayer Group, Penny published a newsletter, Mary's Mantle, for 25 years with a subscribing readership of over 5,000. Mary's Mantle expounded on Our Lady's messages, featuring prominent articles about healing – both physical and spiritual – and beautiful testimonies of conversion through Our Lady's reported apparitions.

Several prayer groups were started by Penny and (always) a priest, along with a small group of friends who had experienced Medjugorje together. Four prayer groups met monthly, meeting from 1986 until 2013 praying on First Fridays for vocations, families, world peace, and an end to abortion.

Penny was a guest of Monsignor Tom Hartman's Rockville Centre Diocese's Network, Telecare, back in 1987 and the 1990's sharing about her experience in bringing internationally known close friend and prayer partner, Detective Steven McDonald, to Medjugorje. Steven became a quadriplegic after being shot in NY's Central Park in 1986.

In 2014, Penny co-produced a documentary about the reported apparitions of Medjugorje entitled "God Exists... The Queen of Peace Speaks from Medjugorje." Penny's film was written and produced by Peter Powell, a researcher and cinematographer who had worked on more than 150 media campaigns in the USA and overseas. Penny's narrator was Rita Gam, a veteran actress, who was under contract with MGM studios. Over 3,000 copies of Penny's documentary have been distributed, and it remains available on Amazon.

Penny's life took a drastic turn when she was very far away from her faith. The pain of her younger brother's suicide brought Penny to her knees. Her conversion story, *Medjugorje...My Lifelong Journey with Our Lady*, was inspired by Fr. Svetazor Kraljevic, OFM, in Medjugorje. In her book, Penny takes the reader from her darkest days of losing her closest friend, through stages of surrender, and finally drawing closer to Jesus by way of Our Lady's messages from Medjugorje.

Penny has been married to Michael for 50 years. She is the mother of three children and grandmother of six and currently lives in Lynbrook, NY.

To learn more about Penny Abbruzzese's work for Our Lady, you can obtain a copy of the Documentary, "*God Exists…The Queen of Peace Speaks from Medjugorje*" (see next page) through Amazon or email Penny at

pennyabb@aol.com

God Exists

The Queen of Peace
Speaks from Medjugorje...

written and produced by PETER POWELL | narrated by RITA GAM |
co-producers PENNY ABBRUZZESE & MATE T. VASILJ | edited by MARIA TERESA ALVARADO |
Music composer LISA CUNNINGHAM © OUR LADY QUEEN OF PEACE PRAYER GROUP, 2013

Made in the USA
Monee, IL
26 September 2022